THE STILL ARROW

THE ITALIAN LIST

THE STILL ARROW

THREE ATTEMPTS TO ANNUL TIME

ELVIO FACHINELLI

TRANSLATED BY LORENZO CHIESA

LONDON NEW YORK CALCUTTA

SERIES EDITOR: ALBERTO TOSCANO

Seagull Books, 2021

Originally published in 1979 as
Elvio Fachinelli, *La freccia ferma: Tre tentativi di annullare il tempo*
© Adelphi Edizioni, Milan, 1992

First published in English translation by Seagull Books, 2021
English translation © Lorenzo Chiesa, 2021

ISBN 978 0 8574 2 851 6

British Library Cataloguing-in-Publication Data
A catalogue record for this book is available from the British Library

Typeset by Seagull Books, Calcutta, India
Printed and bound in the USA by Integrated Books International

CONTENTS

Zénon! Cruel Zénon! Zénon d'Élée!
M'as-tu percé de cette flèche ailée
Qui vibre, vole, et qui ne vole pas!

Zeno! Cruel Zeno! Zeno of Elea!
Have you pierced my flesh with your winged arrow,
Which quivers, flies, yet does not seem to fly?

P. VALÉRY, 'Cimetière marin' /
'The Cemetery by the Sea'[1]

1 Paul Valéry, 'The Cemetery by the Sea' (Howard Moss trans.), *The Sewanee Review* 71(3) (Summer 1963): 464.

Preface

This investigation originates from within psychoanalytic experience, as the first effect of my surprise at the behaviour of the person I will here call 'the man who annulled time'. I am therefore indebted to him for the reflections I have now gathered together and which are dedicated to him.

As the reader will observe, they are almost entirely devoid of psychoanalytic terminology. This is the case not only because the latter has become entrenched in hypostatized formulas—in both specialized and common use—that often hinder, rather than facilitate, the understanding of concrete situations; but especially because, following the thread of discovery, I was obliged to go beyond the psychoanalytic field and deal with other problems which are formulated differently. However, the reader will observe how there is a continuous connection between the inside and outside; this connection is also reflected in the more strictly psychoanalytic problems. For example, questioning time and the ways in which it is elaborated directly concerns the time of and in psychoanalysis. This topic, which is in my view central to the future of psychoanalysis and its interventions, has so far mostly been neglected. To the point that, without being too unfair, we could regard psychoanalysis as another attempt to annul time . . . I hope to be able to return to this issue in the near future.

Some of the paragraphs in the book are in italics in order to distinguish them from the rest. They are interventions in the text, or more problematic suggestions. Ultimately, they indicate a kind of second-order with regard to the general line of my investigation.

Armenistis
Summer 1979

*

I wish to thank Magda Esposito, Andrea Sabbadini, Fausto Petrella, Sergio Benvenuto, Valentina Fortichiari, Paolo Volponi, Gabriella Buzzatti, Enzo Morpurgo, Maria Pingitore, and Roberto Orefice for the suggestions, indications, and criticism they offered me on various occasions.

I
THE MAN WHO ANNULLED TIME[1]

This is what happens, one day in the winter of 1977, in a big Italian city, to a forty-five-year-old small businessman:

THE DIFFICULT APPOINTMENT

He has to meet a lawyer to show him some documents about his tax returns. He is given an appointment at 18.30. He asks to postpone it by one hour because he first needs to see his analyst. The appointment is therefore postponed to around 19.30. After that, he grows increasingly uncertain: his wife won't be back home from the office by then, so how can he go to the lawyer?

Does his wife have to accompany him? No, that's not the case. The documents he wants to show the lawyer are on a shelf at home; just the other day, his wife put the weekly magazine *Il Mondo* on top of them. Glancing at its cover, he seems to have seen the following masthead, 'Supplement of the "Corriere della Sera"', or something like that. That is to say, the supplement of a daily, something he cannot read, because dailies come out on Sundays too, and *working on Sundays is a mortal sin.* Touching the magazine to extract the documents from beneath it would equally be a mortal sin. If his wife were home, he could ask her to carry out the forbidden action. But his wife will not be at home by 19.00 or even by 19.30.

He contemplates phoning the lawyer to postpone the appointment. But that's not possible. He is the one who accepted the appointment earlier, and the lawyer will think he's crazy. He therefore needs

1 A first draft of this chapter was presented and discussed at a seminar of the Associazione di Psicoterapia Critica that took place in Milan in May 1978 and published in Andrea Sabbadini (ed.), *Il tempo in psicoanalisi* [Time in Psychoanalysis] (Milan: Feltrinelli, 1979), pp. 175–90.

to decide to extract the documents himself and go to the lawyer. After that, he will perform the 'annulment'.

The 'annulment' amounts to the following: he will repeat *in reverse order* every action he carried out from the moment he extracted the documents. Leaving the lawyer's office, he will come down the stairs turned upwards, drive his car in reverse until he reaches his house, then climb the stairs looking downwards. Finally, he will reach the shelf from which he took the documents and place them exactly in the position they were in before by making a gesture opposite to the one he made when he took them. At that point, the sinful action will have been 'annulled'.

This particular way of proceeding, which I have here described in a very simplified manner, is part of a general obsessive way of life about which I will now write in detail.

A LIFE ACCORDING TO MOSES

From the moment he wakes up in the morning to the moment he falls asleep at night, *everything* must be carried out according to a 'system' of meticulous and complicated rules; so much so that, in order to elude it, he spends most of the day sitting in front of the television, having 'renounced' almost everything. His simplest movement—moving an arm, standing up or taking a few steps—involves the obligation to comply with so many precise procedures that he prefers to sit, although sitting inertly does not free him from the 'system'. Out of necessity, the elementary functions survive: eating, defecating, urinating; but these are themselves made endless by the rules of compliance. Sexual activity is reduced to some masturbation (following his 'reasoning': if I forbid that too, I might as well die). He only goes out when he visits the swimming pool—but he does not always get there in time—and he has his psychoanalytic sessions (at first, in spite of leaving home with a couple of hours in hand, he could only arrive by the end of the session or after, given the number of rules he had to follow to get in the car, drive, follow a compulsory itinerary, climb the stairs to my office). Some extra 'movement' became necessary when he began his psychoanalysis due to its cost: he met the managers of the company of which he is a shareholder, his trusted lawyer, etc. Even the activity of putting on his clothes is incredibly hampered: at times, he ends up going out with his trousers unzipped and shoes untied. The same happens with shaving, and cutting his hair.

What imposes this kind of life on him is, explicitly, Moses' Decalogue, but one that is extraordinarily stretched and ramified beyond its literal statements. For example, the Sixth Commandment enjoins us not to commit impure acts. But the impure act has lost its substantiality and delimitation; hence saying the word *yellow* is an impure act because *yellow* evokes *lemon*, and *lemon* evokes *limonare* [snogging] . . . Or: one must observe Sundays as holy days, the days of the Lord. But also Mondays, because they are contiguous with Sundays, and Tuesdays . . . In this way, periods comprising whole weeks and months are established during which it is impossible to do anything, because they are devoted to the Lord.

THE SEGMENTATION OF TIME

Despite the loss of its concreteness and its movement along these bizarre mental paths, the law has not mitigated its rigour; rather, it tenaciously detects sin in every remote allusion, following threads and ramifications that are increasingly tenuous and distant. Here the law is mercilessly and threateningly active while, paradoxically, its rigour is attenuated precisely at the starting point where concrete sinning is at stake. For example, thanks to a 'reasoning' based on survival, he has preserved masturbation. Moreover, precisely because of his observances, he regularly ends up not going to Mass on Sundays.

At this point, having been banished in every direction, action, word, and thought, sin and evil turn out to be omnipresent. The simplest remedy to avoid sin is suppressing actions, words and thoughts. But there is a non-eliminable *remainder*—inevitable actions, words and thoughts.

With respect to this remainder, the task is therefore to carry it out in a way that does not break the law. For instance, stepping out of bed, he will touch the ground with the right foot (in keeping with the fact that, because of mental connections, the right is good and the left is evil). But already within this simple act are present different possibilities; that is to say, the evil alternative as opposed to the good is presented again at every moment—at every moment, there is a proper behaviour as opposed to a forbidden one.

The result of this continuous alternative is the splitting up, or segmentation, of concrete time—of time as the flux and individual form of action—into a series of timelets [*tempuscoli*] that are increasingly smaller. Each of them is separated and isolated from the others, for the purpose of carrying out the corresponding segment of action in the correct way and keeping it distinct from the subsequent timelet in which the alternative arises again. Time is segmented according to a tendency to infinity, in connection with the tendency for evil to infinitely present itself. Each action, which is already as such residual, is fragmented into a series of increasingly smaller acts and thus becomes incredibly lengthy and arduous.

ZENO'S MAN

We could say that this obsessive procedure embodies, with respect to time, one of the aporias about motion stated by Zeno of Elea. The first of them, as reported by Aristotle, declares that 'if motion exists, it is necessary that what moves covers infinite segments in a finite time; but this is impossible, hence motion does not exist'. Zeno's demonstration is as follows: 'What moves must cover a given distance; but insofar as each distance is infinitely divisible, what moves must first travel half the distance it has to cover and then its entirety. But prior to covering half the distance, it must travel half of that half, and again half of the latter. But if halves are infinite, since it is possible to take half of each segment one has already taken, then it is impossible to cover infinite segments in a finite time'.[2] *In this way, in true reality—the one that is not apparent—the arrow fired from Zeno's bow stands still at the point of departure.*

2 I am here quoting Simplicius' exposition (*Physics*, 1013, 4), which is longer and clearer than Aristotle's rather concise account.

We saw that this procedure of division or dichotomy is also present in our obsessional. In order to carry out a given action, a certain amount of time is needed. But insofar as time is infinitely divisible, it is impossible to carry out the action. So, from this standpoint, the obsessional is a living demonstration of the impossibility of acting due to a division of time that tends to be endless; for him too, the shot arrow—immobilized by the infinity of time instead of that of space—never reaches its target. (Actually, the division concerns the unfolding of action in time, just as, in Zeno's case, it concerned the motion of that which moves in space; by way of simplification, we can speak of a division of time and space.)

In Zeno, the demonstration intends to support and defend—against the disdain of his contemporaries—Parmenides' notion of 'being', of the 'all is one'[3]*—as non-generated, everlasting, undivided, immobile and so on . . . Parmenides' 'being' corresponds to a 'word-truth-reality' that excludes from itself what 'is not', and thus also what 'was' and 'will be'. In other words, it is eternal not in the sense that the present is added to a past and future infinite, but as a present that excludes from itself every past and future, precisely as happens with the grammatical tense.*[4] *We could therefore suggest that an immobility frozen in time and space defends itself through Zeno's arguments; just as in the case of the obsessional, the operations aimed at the most perfect performance of an action actually entail its likely exclusion, and the reaffirmation of a state of immutability and immobility in the present. There is neither past nor future but a 'stationary' condition within a permanent restlessness.*

Moreover, in both cases, we are dealing with operations conducted on enemy ground and compromises with what must be rejected; philosophical critique has already noticed this with regard to Zeno;[5] *it also turns out to be evident in the analysis of our obsessional.*

3 Plato, *Parmenides*, 127e–128e.

4 Guido Calogero, *Storia della logica antica* [History of Ancient Logic], VOL. 1 (Bari: Laterza, 1967), p. 134.

5 Calogero, *Storia della logica antica*, pp. 179–82. See also Giorgio Colli, *La nascita della filosofia* [The Birth of Philosophy] (Milan: Adelphi, 1975), pp. 89–93. According to Colli, in spite of his effort to safeguard the 'divine matrix' of Parmenides' thought, Zeno disobeyed his teacher and followed to the extreme consequences 'the destructive path of non-being, that is, dialectical reasoning'.

SERIES, CEREMONIAL, MORAL MACHINE

Moving from these premises, we can grasp the improper use of the term 'ceremonial' which is usually employed to describe this kind of behaviour. It can justifiably be applied to a moment of crystallization and immobility on the path of temporal segmentation; here it indeed has the aspect and almost the rhythm of a series of pre-established acts, performed in an absolutely rigorous way in pursuit of a goal. But the 'system' does not stop ramifying, and thus ends up overwhelming the series and its unfolding. We should instead speak of a behaviour and time of observance, and of obedience of the law, that pulsates in opposition to the omnipresent evil.

What is the limit of this process? There is no internal limit; it is an infinite process, just as the succession of thoughts and the hunt for evil that take place within it are themselves infinite. The interruptions and pauses are provisional. For example, when one is physically exhausted—when one says 'Enough, I can't bear it, God cannot want this from me!'—there is a moment of relief. But this is only in order to enable the process to resume later, at times even more intensely. Or consider when external life—the life of everybody else—pops into the obsessional's head alongside thoughts of everything he has had to renounce; there is a shock, an attempt to grab hold again of something he let slip through his fingers. Or, we could say, when the law itself allows an internal stratagem or trick that leads to a containment of obligatory actions and their condensation. It is a 'system within a system', so to speak. If, for instance, a series of actions can be performed only 'once a day', then a kind of protection is constructed against their endless segmentation, because otherwise one would initiate the emergence of 'other times'. But in every case the problem of infringement rapidly arises and, along with it, that of 'annulment'.

The latter should now be clearer. Time is segmented into a series of timelets, each enclosed and delimited within itself. A 'now' follows another 'now'. If an infringement or non-compliance happens in one 'now', this means that the atom of time was not concluded in the right way and is opened onto the subsequent one and all the others, radically involving them in evil. While the law segments time into a series of individual imperative acts, the evil it fights tends to expand forward and, so to speak, involve—starting from just one breaching point—the entire course of actions. The law constitutes a sectioned and divided time; evil reconstitutes a consecutive time which enables in its continuity a *history*, although it is an entirely negative and guilty one. The 'now' and 'now' of the law—which are points isolated from one another—are replaced by a 'now' connected with all the subsequent 'afters' of evil. Whence the necessity, in the 'annulment', to proceed to close again all the timelets that have become negative, to repeat or repair in reverse order the segments of corresponding actions. And from here too follows the fundamental importance of not letting pass too much time or too many actions, otherwise the task becomes exhausting and impossible.

Moreover, we should bear in mind that the more apparently insignificant (and easy to rectify) the sinful action, the greater the sense of urgency in what concerns its reparation. If in fact it is a matter 'beyond human strength', it becomes inevitable to give up; but in every other case—for example, putting a magazine back in its place—the requirement for annulment becomes irrepressible. Clearly a number of impossibilities soon appear everywhere: repeating everything one said backwards; making one's urine re-enter the body; vomiting what is already digested. It is only by means of a meticulous and anguishing examination that the obsessional is able to determine up to what point he must go and where instead he must give up, replacing the impossible action with a condensed simulacrum of action that functions as its equivalent.

The set of these operations tends to establish a serial time, without history, an infinite collection of 'nows'. The force of evil continuously opposes this—weakly, but without interruption, it opposes such a segmented time with a unitary time in which the present of the 'now' is connected with the future of the 'after', albeit in a totally negative and guilt-ridden way. The first kind of time is reversible, mechanical and precise; the second is irreversible, and increasingly unrestrained and anguishing. The first tends to prevail; the second becomes imperceptible but never fully disappears. Life, in the common sense of the word, almost vanishes or is reduced to a few besieged islands; what prevails is the impersonal pulse of a kind of *moral machine* that almost completely occupies the horizon. Life is continuously postponed to a 'tomorrow' that will never come, because the pulse of the machine is ceaseless.

FROM ABSOLUTE MODELS TO THE WC

This is the outcome of a process that has been going on for more than thirty years, from early adolescence to full maturity.[6] We should now ask why and how it was established. In the first place, this can be deduced from observing the procedure and functioning of the machine itself. We can infer the meaning of its intervention from the kind of operations that are carried out. Here are some extremely banal examples. Our friend cannot put on a belt. Why? Because . . . because it is an unnecessary surplus object . . . and using unnecessary objects is an index of vanity, and vanity is a serious sin . . . *but it does not stop there*, and so we learn that he has always had an intense desire to be elegant, impressive, to stand out; the support for this is the model of a man 'on top of things' [*in gamba*], an elegant lady-killer of sorts, a model proposed by his mother when he was a child. Another example. During the day, he is very worried by the WC problem: it is absolutely necessary that the toilet lid be up; putting the lid down is a sin. Why? Because . . . because putting the toilet lid down is like shutting doors, a sin . . . and it is a sin because shutting doors means considering others as thieves, and this is a sin . . . *from here one moves on* to the problem of attacking and criticizing others,

6 Its full development was certainly favoured by the subject's economic status, which quite easily made him avoid the common requirements of earning, competition, and so on. All in all, he could avoid the pressure of linear historical-economical time; but his economic status favoured or permitted the process—it did *not* determine it.

dominating them, which many years ago was a haunting problem for him; a man 'on top of things' is a resolute man, imperious and frank in his opinions and criticisms, like his father.[7]

In both these examples we thus have a series of equivalences between objects and situations that, according to common opinion, are of a very different order. In both cases, these equivalences go through a *common point*—sin—and overcome it. Belt = unnecessary object = vanity, sin = trying to impress, showing off, standing out. WC = shutting doors = criticizing others, sin = being assertive, dominating. For our obsessional, these equivalences are now all included in the general category of sin, with the further specification that the first term (the belt; the WC) is far more challenging than the last (being a man 'on top of things'). But it is easy to see how, chronologically, these equivalences were established *after* the failed solution of some fundamental problems of personal identity with respect to *proposed models*. The term that now appears as last, and almost detached from the series of equivalences—atonic and indifferent like an insignificant 'memory'—was the first in reality, the matrix of his difficulties.

At the beginning of his story, many years ago, there was a relationship with models proposed by unquestioned authorities; these images became internal and, it would seem, strong enough to absorb him almost entirely and make him feel hesitant and useless in face of the tasks of his own identity and affirmation. His are *parents-models*, in every sense; they function as absolute precedents; he thinks that only by living up to them will he be able to preserve their love and esteem (he's an only child). But in order to live up to them, he should be able to assess, confront and criticize them. Now, how is it possible to assess an authority that, for him, is placed at a higher level—

7 In a dream the relation between 'toilet lid up' and the virile position is further specified: *the toilet lid cannot stay up, it's as if it were made of soft plastic, and he finds himself beside the bed of a man, with the feeling of being a woman.* In his associations, the plastic toilet lid immediately refers to the penis that cannot stay up, to the problem of a choice between passive and active tendencies, etc.

already by definition—and, at the same time, inside him, as a part of him? There emerges an unsolvable dilemma: he desires to affirm himself, but affirming oneself entails the decision to face a series of risks. First of all, the risk of distancing himself from these models, so as to make them assessable and tangible for the first time; given that they are embodied in him, distancing himself from them means *striking* at the same time both them and himself, running the risk of losing their love and his self-love. Affirming oneself thus becomes a difficult decision, a decision both violent and guilty.

THE IMPERSONAL CONFLICT

Facing this dilemma, at a certain point there arises an apparent solution. At the age of around twelve or thirteen, he is sent to a strict and prestigious Jesuits' college where religious education is based on precepts and catechism. Thanks to the observance of the Commandments, required by the new authority, it seems he is given the possibility of solving his dilemma. He will scrupulously observe the Commandments, and this impersonal observance will work as a guarantee, pledge and magical protection for every project concerning his life. In this way, the problem of his autonomous choices is no longer directly at stake. What is in question is obeying a higher and external agency: this enables him to repeat, on a more remote level, the position of the child entrusted to an adult while appearing to grant him a chance to access adult life.

What is essential is thus moved to a well-defined ground (that of 'sin') with respect to which there exists an equally defined system of rules—in other words, an elementary ethical system. The immediate and short-term advantage of this repositioning consists in the depersonalization of the conflict; he is no longer exposed to the risks of personal decisions, whose stakes nonetheless seem to him to be ensured by his new obedience. The disadvantage—which will soon turn out to be massive—is that, in this way, the previously concrete and immediate conflict becomes abstract and indirect. However, the sense of guilt does not diminish; it simply moves from self-realization to the content of individual sins. In brief, having abandoned its strictly personal terms, the conflict is in fact presented again with regard to the terms of religious law and then, gradually, to the various ideational derivatives of sin—of which we saw some examples.

All in all, what takes place is that hunt for evil enacted by the machine of the law, which entails the mutation of time we have already described. We should observe that the moral machine becomes ever stronger not out of its own strength and growth but out of a simple expansion of the void—because the *subject of life*, by which I mean the centre of personal life, withdraws and contracts itself as it confronts the machine. While, on the one hand, concretely realizing oneself in an autonomous way is no longer a fundamental problem—at times it is not even a problem but only a 'memory'—on the other, the machine prevails and the subject of life tends to be confused with the *subject of the moral machine*. There thus emerges that (occasionally very intense) identification with the obsessive 'system', which is here particularly clear-cut, since the 'system' coincides at bottom with the commandments of ordinary religion. The lack of concrete social realization is therefore substituted with a realization in the guise of being the founder, minister and faithful follower of the *true religion*. At this point, what is usually lived and described as the 'oppression' exerted by the system—the implacable machine—almost becomes an omnipotent self-realization. The obsessional does not become God but participates in His omnipotence.

FREUD AND THE FREUDIANS

The term 'annulment'—as well as 'system' and 'system within a system'—is not derived from psychoanalytic readings or the analyst's words. It was the subject himself who coined it in order to designate the procedure that corrects infringements. It should be stressed that the procedure of segmentation and isolation of time was not given a name, which seems to make it correspond to a level of more immediate spontaneity, one that is not perceived reflexively. After all, the whole set of the rules of obedience along with the objects to which they are applied is itself unfolded on a non-reflexive plane. The procedure of 'annulment' stands out for the subject himself because it is by far the most excruciating and dreaded of all procedures.

It is now necessary to clarify the relation between this procedure and the 'defensive process' Freud identifies and describes as *Ungeschehenmachen*, 'undoing what has been done', or 'retroactive annulment'. His first references to this concept appear to be in the case of the *Rat Man* (1909):

> On the day of her departure he knocked his foot against a stone lying in the road, and was *obliged* to put it out of the way by the side of the road, because the idea struck him that her carriage would be driving along the same road in a few hours' time and might come to grief against the stone. But a few minutes later it occurred to him that this was absurd, and he was *obliged* to go back and replace the stone in its original position in the middle of the road.[8]

According to Freud,

> a battle between love and hate was raging in the lover's breast, and the object of both these feelings was one and the same person. The battle was represented in a plastic form by his compulsive and symbolic act of removing the stone from the road along which she was to drive, and then of undoing this deed of love by replacing the stone where it had lain, so that her carriage might come to grief against it and she herself be hurt.[9]

We are therefore dealing with one of those 'compulsive acts, in two successive stages, of which the second neutralizes the first',[10] and

8 Sigmund Freud, 'Notes upon a Case of Obsessional Neurosis' in *The Standard Edition of the Complete Works of Sigmund Freud*, VOL. 10 (London: Vintage, 2001), p. 190. See also Freud, *Gesammelte Werke*, VOL. 7 (London: Imago Publishing, 1940), p. 412. [Henceforth, *SE* and *GW*, respectively.]

9 Freud, 'A Case of Obsessional Neurosis', p. 191 / *GW*, VOL. 7, p. 414.

10 Freud, 'A Case of Obsessional Neurosis', p. 192 / *GW*, VOL. 7, p. 414.

in which two opposite impulses—love and hatred—can be satisfied one after the other. (We should highlight how, in this initial clinical description, Freud uses two different verbs—*rückgänging machen*, 'to revoke', 'to reverse a change' and *aufheben*, 'to remove'—for the procedure the Italian translation equally renders as *annullare*, 'to annul'.)[11]

In 1925, Freud returned more extensively to this issue in *Inhibition, Symptom and Anxiety*, and every subsequent psychoanalytic reflection took up the question from here. 'Undoing what has been done' (the definitive term is *Ungeschehenmachen*) does not appear only in diphasic symptoms, as was the case in the 1909 description; it also constitutes one of the sources of the obsessional ceremonial, and explains the compulsion to repeat; in any case, it is also broadly used in magical actions, popular customs and religious ceremonies.[12] As we can see, the notion runs the risk of becoming eclectic and all-embracing, since Freud does not seem to be concerned with telling us what unifies (or is the common element among) these different experiences. In my opinion, the reason for this is perhaps that, in this text, Freud aims at framing this procedure within the 'defensive process' or 'mechanism of defence'—a term he takes up here after more than thirty years.[13] Now, I think this interpretative schema in terms of defence is insufficient when confronted with the variety of situations in which it can be found. After all, Freud hints in passing at the fact that, by means of this procedure, 'the neurotic person will try to make the past itself non-existent' (the verb he uses here is again *aufheben*).[14] Undoing what has been done therefore pertains to the ways in which one treats and elaborates time; it is a *temporal technique*

11 [The English translation also uses two different verbs: 'to undo' and 'to neutralize'—Trans.]

12 Sigmund Freud, 'Inhibition, Symptom and Anxiety' in *SE*, VOL. 20 (1925–1926), pp. 118–19 / *GW*, VOL. 14, pp. 149–50.

13 Freud, 'Inhibition, Symptom and Anxiety', pp. 162–3 / *GW*, VOL. 14, pp. 195–7.

14 Freud, 'Inhibition, Symptom and Anxiety', p. 119 / *GW*, VOL. 14, p. 150.

and, in my view, this alone can be the common element among the various experiences in which we find it at work.

To the best of my knowledge, later psychoanalysts have not specifically considered the procedure of *Ungeschehenmachen*—unlike 'isolation', which, as we saw earlier, is strictly linked with it.[15] Anna Freud directly refers to her father's works and lists annulment among the various mechanisms of defence.[16] Fenichel further extends the number of cases, which now also include the 'magic of symmetry'.[17] Lewin thinks it is active in dreams.[18]

At this stage, it seems appropriate to ask whether the procedure we described earlier corresponds to those indicated by Freud and the other scholars we mentioned, or better, whether it requires a series of further considerations. In fact, we can grasp some basic differences. In the first example provided by Freud, knocking one's foot against a stone prompts the fantasy of an accident; there is a quite clear connection between the real accident, its phantasmatic repercussion and the obsessive procedure; the annulment concerns an isolated act and happens instantaneously. In the situation I described, there is also, originally, a real element—the appointment with the lawyer (connected with that with the analyst). But here we do not have the personalized aggressive fantasy that is derived from the real element in Freud's case. In its place is an abstract problem: sinning against the day of the Lord. The first stage of the action is already on a completely different ground, which has no reference to the

15 See especially Kurt Robert Eissler, 'On Isolation', *The Psychoanalytic Study of the Child* 14 (1959): 29–60, and the discussion of a panel held on the topic in San Francisco in 1958, reported by Henry F. Marasse, *Journal of the American Psychoanalytic Association* 7 (1959): 163–72.

16 Anna Freud, *The Ego and the Mechanisms of Defence* (London: Karnac Books, 1993), p. 34.

17 Otto Fenichel, *The Psychoanalytic Theory of Neurosis* (London: Routledge, 1996), p. 154.

18 Bertram D. Lewin, 'Anal Eroticism and the Mechanism of Undoing', *Psychoanalytic Quarterly* 1 (1932): 343–4.

initial concrete situation: what is at stake is moving a newspaper supplement. The annulment of such a simple act is not instantaneous but involves the annulment of every act that follows it.

We are therefore facing something more than a complication. Rather, we obtain the full development of a situation that was only outlined in Freud's case. And this development is intimately linked to the use of a series of temporal procedures that are thoroughly peculiar. An independent world is thus formed, one that has its own time which is apparently fully unbound and autonomous from ordinary time.

VON GEBSATTEL

I say *apparently* because what emerges here is a most serious disagreement with the scholars who have dealt in depth with this kind of world from a phenomenological (or 'anthropo-analytic') standpoint. First and foremost, we should single out Viktor Emil von Gebsattel, the author of the well-known 'Die Welt des Zwangskranken'.[19] In this text, von Gebsattel himself relies on fully developed obsessive situations; observing the manifestation of these alien worlds, he is led to detect an incessant battle against something that from the outset is radically different from common experience, namely, the 'anti-eidos'—understood as a set of forces that are opposed to any form, directed towards the dissolution of form, and specified at each turn, in a secondary way, as impure, dirty, sinful and so on.[20]

Now, this is the most evident aspect that obsessive behaviour presents us with. But it is *never* a pure 'bursting forth of primitive ways of perceiving';[21] even in the most extreme cases, it is never disconnected from the terms of the real conflict that preceded it temporally; instead, it continues to coexist with such a conflict.

19 Viktor Emil von Gebsattel, 'Die Welt des Zwangskranken' in *Prolegomena einer medizinischen Anthropologie* (Berlin: Springer-Verlag, 1954), pp. 74–128.

20 von Gebsattel, 'Die Welt des Zwangskranken', p. 122.

21 von Gebsattel, 'Die Welt des Zwangskranken', p. 123.

This can be demonstrated in various ways. First of all, as I pointed out, the obsessive situation takes the form of a development, and it is possible to grasp—both within the same person and among different people—various levels of relationship with shared reality, which are increasingly more distant and indirect. For instance, in the case of a young person, it is not difficult to grasp the immediate link between obsessive ideas about death and his relationship with paternal authority. The obsessive world has, so to speak, not yet left home, that is, it has not yet become fully depersonalized. After decades into an obsessive 'career'—as in the situation we are dealing with—these kinds of links are less detectable, because an intermediate barrier of an abstract-generic kind (mortal 'sin') has been erected from which the vicissitudes of obsessive thinking seem to flow autonomously.

But even in these extreme situations there is a reference to the real conflict, at least in *dreams*. It is curious that, despite his carefulness, von Gebsattel did not question the destiny of the 'anti-eidos' in dreams and fantasies. If he did, he would have realized how the real conflict is always present there, and more or less connected with the obsessive themes. During the day, the latter can prove to be exclusive and autonomous; but in dreams and fantasies obsessive themes are strictly connected with given historical situations. In dreams, one can witness the actual transcription of the initial conflict into obsessive terms, or the simultaneous presence of the historical conflict and its obsessive translation—as if they were superimposed.

Finally, let me add a third consideration which is intimately bound to the theme of obsession. Von Gebsattel insightfully described—without referring to Freudian 'mechanisms'—the homogenization of obsessive time, the fact that it proceeds in fits and starts according to a 'voluntary fiat'.[22] But he did not notice how, facing this fragmented and serialized time, there is always the consecutive time—attached to the future—of the refused element, that is to say, of the 'anti-eidos'. As we saw, the contamination of actions

22 von Gebsattel, 'Die Welt des Zwangskranken', p. 105.

promoted by the latter constitutes the time of a—at least potential albeit negative and corrupted—history.

In von Gebsattel's 'anti-eidos' we should therefore detect not the 'quintessence of every destroying power'[23] but the intermediate barrier, of an abstract-generic nature, which the obsessional constructs as a first external bastion against the difficulty posed by choices and personal decisions. These difficulties are also deeply embedded in the subject's eros. It is in fact no coincidence that sexuality is constantly underestimated in von Gebsattel's work, even in transparent ways. For instance, describing the case of a girl for whom the beginning of the syndrome coincides with religious education and develops for some time as an obsession of impurity, he refers to what she says as follows: 'When I went to church and the garter came loose, the hand that put it back in place became impure, and also the little prayer book which I had taken with that hand'. According to von Gebsattel, here 'we are not dealing with a sexual matter, but only with what is linked with physiological needs'.[24] Precisely insofar as one underestimates its conflicts, reality itself tends to flicker only as something distant, ideally pure and happy. For the obsessional this is indeed the case, but precisely because he buried his conflicts and considers them to be dead while in fact he lives with them daily in each of his gestures. After noticing the obsessional's tendency to literality, von Gebsattel took the obsessional literally with regard to sexuality and reality.

A THEORETICAL PROBLEM

In Freud and von Gebsattel, we are facing clearly divergent theoretical positions with respect to obsessive phenomena. Freud—and I am here referring not only to his observations on annulment but also to his writings specifically devoted to obsessional neurosis—does not question the qualitative change and leap in the passage from the personal conflict to its obsessive transcription; nor does he question the

23 von Gebsattel, 'Die Welt des Zwangskranken', p. 127.

24 von Gebsattel, 'Die Welt des Zwangskranken', p. 91 ff.

passage from the time of the conflict to the particular kind of obsessive time, an extreme example of which we have provided here—or only in a peripheral way.

For Freud, there is an uninterrupted continuity between obsessive terms and the personal history of the same situation. Indeed, in the psychoanalytic process, we see them appearing together in so-called free associations—as in the previous example about the belt and the WC. But we are obliged to acknowledge an extraordinary qualitative gap between, say, the problem of the belt and the contiguous one about appearing and standing out in public. The belt amounts to an impoverished and derisory situation, but only for those who look at it from the outside, from the standpoint of the personal conflict. Instead, for those who live it daily from the inside, it essentially partakes of a situation that is both terrible and fascinating, which in codified terms we could easily call sacred. *This is what Freud systematically overlooks. The connection between immediate and obsessive problems is undeniable; but it is equally undeniable that this nexus and sequence has undergone a phase shift, which is correlated to an equally clear temporal change.*

On the other hand, as we saw, von Gebsattel grasps this other world but, in a symmetrical and opposite way, he radically isolates it from its context which is for him basically devoid of importance and interest. We should add that he is also concerned not to ask embarrassing questions to the world traditionally defined as sacred from the standpoint of this gloomy and 'pathological' anti-eidos.[25]

In their absoluteness and partiality, these two positions seem to indicate that there is here a fundamental theoretical problem that still remains unsolved. We will return to it later after examining other forms of time annulment—such a detour is necessary.

25 von Gebsattel, 'Die Welt des Zwangskranken', p. 93.

II
PULSE, WHEEL, ARROW

THE DIVINE PULSATION

In a basic formulation, the annulment of time takes the shape of an order, 'not now!', by means of which a corresponding timely event, 'now!', is annulled in its immediate connection with the subject that carries out the annulment.

If the event can be annulled, in virtue of the same mastery over time, this necessarily implies that the event can also be directly recreated in a timely fashion. In its simplest formulation, the annulment is thus coupled with its opposite—a 'not now!' is coupled with a 'now!'

We therefore obtain an acting on time that is immediately located on two antithetical sides, both of which are available to the sovereign subject. If this acting on time is unfolded according to a regular alternation of 'now!' and 'not now!', we then obtain a pulsation, an elementary rhythmic trend, akin to the game of a god who, tapping his foot, creates and destroys the universe he masters.

THE CHILD-GOD

The child Freud speaks about in *Beyond the Pleasure Principle* comes close to this dimension. His observation is by now classical, but one usually quotes it only in part, that is, the episode of the wooden reel. Let us read what Freud writes *in its entirety*:

> The child was not at all precocious in his intellectual development. At the age of one and a half he could say only a few comprehensible words; he could also make use of a number of sounds which expressed a meaning intelligible to those around him. He was, however, on good terms with

his parents and their one servant-girl, and tributes were paid to his being a 'good boy'. He did not disturb his parents at night, he conscientiously obeyed orders not to touch certain things or go into certain rooms, and above all he never cried when his mother left him for a few hours. At the same time, he was greatly attached to his mother, who had not only fed him herself but had also looked after him without any outside help. This good little boy, however, had an occasional disturbing habit of taking any small objects he could get hold of and throwing them away from him into a corner, under the bed, and so on, so that hunting for his toys and picking them up was often quite a business. As he did this he gave vent to a loud, long-drawn-out 'o-o-o-o', accompanied by an expression of interest and satisfaction. His mother and the writer of the present account were agreed in thinking that this was not a mere interjection but represented the German word 'fort' ['gone']. I eventually realized that it was a game and that the only use he made of any of his toys was to play 'gone' with them.[1] One day I made an observation which confirmed my view. The child had a wooden reel with a piece of string tied round it. It never occurred to him to pull it along the floor behind him, for instance, and play at its being a carriage. What he did was to hold the reel by the string and very skilfully throw it over the edge of his curtained cot, so that it disappeared into it, at the same time uttering his expressive 'o-o-o-o'. He then pulled the reel out of the cot again by the string and hailed its reappearance with a joyful 'da' ['there']. This, then, was the complete game—disappearance and return. As a rule one only witnessed its first act, which was repeated untiringly as a game in itself, though there is no doubt that the greater pleasure was attached to the second act.[2]

1 Literally, *fortsein*, 'being away, absent'.

2 Sigmund Freud, 'Beyond the Pleasure Principle' in *SE*, VOL. 18 (1920–1922), pp. 14–15 / *GW*, VOL. 13, pp. 11–12.

At this point Freud adds a footnote:

> A further observation subsequently confirmed this interpretation fully. One day the child's mother had been away for several hours and on her return was met with the words 'Baby o-o-o!' which was at first incomprehensible. It soon turned out, however, that during this long period of solitude the child had found a method of making himself disappear. He had discovered his reflection in a full-length mirror which did not quite reach to the ground, so that by crouching down he could make his mirror-image 'gone'.[3]

Making the toys, the wooden reel, and finally his own image disappear and return, the child becomes the absolute master of absence and presence, of the 'not now!' and 'now!'. Knowing what the absence-presence at stake amounts to (the toy, the wooden reel, the mother—as Freud believes—or the child himself) is here for us relatively insignificant. What matters instead is stressing the creation, in a concrete life situation, of that pulsation and rhythmical action in two stages, which, as noted, is the simplest action of the god of time.[4]

The child makes an object or his own image disappear and simultaneously utters a sound; he summons what disappeared and utters another sound. The movement of the arm or the whole body and the sound that accompanies it are *inherent* components of the act that produces absence-presence; they are neither separable nor eliminable from it. In this sense, the rhythm of physical movement and that of sound entail in the child, as an initial moment, what dancing, chanting and music stand for in every ritual—with equal significance and, obviously, different elaborations.

3 Freud, 'Beyond the Pleasure Principle', p. 15 / *GW*, VOL. 13, p. 12.

4 In Freud, the wooden-reel game is not interpreted univocally and is examined in the context of the tendency to repeat—that is, in relation to a specific temporal form. Such an implication is lost in many of the psychoanalysts who subsequently dealt with this by-now renowned game. For example, Melanie Klein considers it exclusively from the standpoint of sadism and the tendency to reparation. See *The Psycho-Analysis of Children* (New York: Grove Press, 1960).

We can actually proceed with an even more accurate comparison. In Freud's observation, the rhythmic and auditory game of being 'gone' is implicitly opposed to another and more common modality of reaction to the absence of the mother, namely, crying ('and above all he never cried when his mother left him for a few hours'). Hence crying, as a more or less continuous auditory call, is *replaced* in this child by a complex and discontinuous modality. This is the kind of opposition Lévi-Strauss recovers in the myths he examines in *Mythologiques*. Sounds of a discontinuous or, vice versa, continuous kind accompany situations that are presented as opposite with regard to the proximity or conjunction with nature and society. For example, the conjunction of the honey seeker with the object of his search, or that of a woman with a seductive animal—as situations that are both situated 'on the side' of nature—run the risk of disassociating humankind from culture and society: in the myth, the discontinuous sound of knocking the sandals together appears at this point. In the opposite case—of disjunction from nature and conjunction with culture—an exactly opposite continuous sound appears, that of a snake.[5] An independent confirmation of these correlations seems to be provided by the almost universal relationship between percussion and rites of passage.[6] In the child observed by Freud, the 'naturalness' of crying when one feels passive, impotent, and abandoned is thus replaced by a *rhythmic ritual*, in which the abandoned reverses the situation and proves his worth as a master over himself and the other.

There is no reason to force beyond this point the comparison with the myths studied by Lévi-Strauss and the outcomes of anthropological research. However, the fact remains that this isolated Western child recovered on his own—in a gestural and auditory code—one of the oppositions that other kinds of research encounter in the collective field.

5 Claude Lévi-Strauss, *From Honey to Ashes: Introduction to a Science of Mythology, Volume 2* (San Francisco CA: Harper & Row, 1973), pp. 410–11.

6 Rodney Needham, 'Percussion and Transition', *Man* 2(4) (Dec. 1967): 606–14.

THE 'HERE' AND THE 'NOW'

The child has mastered time by means of a rite of disappearance-reappearance. Evidently, in order to be accepted, this statement must not be contradicted by what we know about the concrete development of the characterization of temporal relationships.

Now, in the child, the order of temporal succession is not initially differentiated from the order of spatial succession and 'a first attempt at analysis consists of separating what really coexists from what does not coexist, or what is present from what is absent, by opposing "now" to "not-now"'.[7]

Outside the individual realm,

> even in our modern civilized languages [. . .] it is common to find one and the same word to express both spatial and temporal relations. And still more abundant examples of these relationships are found in the languages of primitive people, which often seem to possess no other means of expressing the temporal idea. The simple local adverbs are used indifferently in a temporal sense, so that, for example, the word for 'here' merges with the word for 'now', the word for 'there' with that for 'earlier' or 'later'. [. . . T]he only essential difference that is grasped and clearly expressed is that between 'now' and 'not-now'—between the immediate present and that which lies 'outside' it.[8]

Subsequently—and before the concept of time is established as a unitary order of temporal and differentiated stages—we observe the opposition between determined temporal forms to which different 'kinds of action' correspond; everything that happens has its own time, qualitatively different from other times. For instance, Semitic languages do not start with the triadic division between past, present

7 Guido Petter, *Lo sviluppo mentale nelle ricerche di Jean Piaget* [Mental Development in Jean Piaget's Research] (Florence: Giunti, 1967), p. 201.

8 Ernst Cassirer, *The Philosophy of Symbolic Forms, Volume One: Language* (New Haven and London: Yale University Press, 1953), pp. 216–17.

and future, but with a bipartition, since they consider only the opposition between complete and incomplete actions.[9]

TIME AS A WHEEL

Is it therefore possible to think that we can recover, in a collective dimension, traces of the pulsation we encountered in the child-god? The alternation of 'now' and 'not-now' involves a non-cumulative time in which the present plummets into nothingness and is regenerated—instantaneously or not, but without the intervention of the burden of the past and the tension of the future. This is thus a *qualitative* time, occupied only by 'kinds of actions' that have a peculiar form of time: a *cyclical*, non-linear time—all in all, a wheel of time instead of an arrow. This cyclical time, which is regularly regenerated, is the time of every archaic civilization of an agricultural-pastoral type.[10]

9 Cassirer, *The Philosophy of Symbolic Forms*, p. 224.

10 The civilizations that cultural anthropology has mostly dealt with so far have been unproblematically defined, until recently, as primitive, in explicit or implicit opposition to a developed or advanced civilization—ours. Researchers have increasingly realized the ideological weight implied by this term; more recent anthropological texts therefore speak of 'primitive' civilizations in inverted commas or 'so-called primitive'. Lévi-Strauss prefers to speak of a 'prior' instead of 'primitive' science (see *The Savage Mind*, London: Weidenfeld and Nicolson, 1966, p. 16). It is easy to ascertain that these expedients do not much improve the situation. After all, every term used so far to globally designate such societies—as different from ours—are loaded with negative connotations: 'barbarians', 'savages', 'primitives'. It thus seems better to resort to the term 'archaic', in the purely positional sense of antecedent to us. This has itself a negative connotation: archaic as old, decrepit, and thus distant, if not inferior, with respect to the *modern* that assesses it. Furthermore, some scholars have used 'archaic' in the sense of 'original', with a strong metaphysical implication (see, for example, Mircea Eliade, *Cosmos and History: The Myth of the Eternal Return*, New York: Harper, 1959). These actual disadvantages seem to me to be compensated—at least in part—by the fact that 'archaic' does not as such entail any simplification, that is, it does not undermine the complexity of the phenomena under consideration, and this is perhaps the strongest requirement in this field. Consequently, I will mostly use

> If we disregard the 'time specialists' who appeared around the time when the first urban settlements were formed, the fundamental concept of duration is apprehended only through the recurrence of produce or operations necessary to life. The calendar of primitive peoples or of farmers, constructed upon mythical time, is a cycle marked by the return of certain game birds or animals, the ripeness of certain plants, the tilling of soil.[11]

At this stage, we need to expand our argument with regard to some fundamental points.

First of all, the death and regeneration of the world do not seem to be symbolic or allusive events for these societies, as they are for us 'moderns'—or better, for us as external and distant observers. Instead, they are real events in the strict sense of the term, whose regularity—which is jeopardized by multiple dangers emerging from chaos—must be ensured in the most rigorous way. The necessary, dutiful and unique way to achieve this end is the ritual, understood as a regulated set of operations—consisting of acts, gestures and words—that averts danger through an appropriate staging or dramatization. The ritual is therefore the typical intervention in a dangerous or uncertain situation of transition that concerns both collective and individual life.[12] And, in this field, every ritual whose efficacy one counts upon is the actual repetition of a mythical event in which the sought-after regularity of life and death was originally

'archaic' in place of what is usually rendered as 'primitive'—with or without inverted commas.

11 André Leroi-Gourhan, *Gesture and Speech* (Cambridge MA: MIT Press, 1993), p. 316.

12 See Pierre Smith, 'Aspects de l'organisation des rites' in Michel Izard and Pierre Smith (eds), *La fonction symbolique. Essais d'anthropologie* (Paris: Gallimard, 1979), pp. 139–70. It should be observed that, for descriptive purposes and following Lévi-Strauss' suggestion to 'study rituals in themselves and for themselves', this article deliberately severs the concrete links that exist between ritual and myth, ritual and religious belief, etc.

established. This actual repetition is a genuine cosmogony, the effective replication of the primordial cosmogony described by myth.[13]

A question now arises concerning the relationship between the subject acting in the ritual and the mythical event. Converging observations by scholars from various orientations indicate that, for archaic man, myth functions as a model or absolute premise, so much so that his life was defined as a 'quotation-like life'; for every significant action, there is the constant search for a mythical model, 'like the toreador [. . .] stepp[ing] back a pace before doing anything'.[14] Reciprocally, every action is significant only insofar as it reproduces and *repeats* this mythical model. However, this is not a determination of a causal or deterministic kind;[15] instead, we are dealing with a 'foundation' of action from which the latter derives in a non-causal way.[16]

The repetition of the mythical hero's behaviour in the ritual is what guarantees the regular course of the universe. Thus the individual's own initiative does not matter; outside ritual observance, it is not only meaningless but amounts to an infringement that needs to be remedied. In archaic people, we therefore have a logic of acting according to rules of observance that are completely different from those of modern action, which is based on logics of exploration, expansion, adventure and conflict.

We should further notice that cyclical time, ideally based in every archaic civilization on celestial motion, intervenes as a central element in the constitution of a:

> system of symbolic representation of the universe which, in broad outline, is astonishingly similar in America, China,

13 Eliade, *The Myth of the Eternal Return*, p. 17 ff.

14 Károly Kerényi, 'Prolegomena' in Carl Gustav Jung and Károly Kerényi, *On a Science of Mythology: The Myth of the Divine Child and the Mysteries of Eleusis* (New York: Pantheon Books, 1949), p. 5.

15 Bronislaw Malinowski, 'Myth in Primitive Psychology' in *Magic, Science, and Religion and Other Essays* (Boston MA: Beacon Press, 1948), pp. 72–124.

16 Kerényi, 'Prolegomena', p. 8.

India, Mesopotamia, Egypt, and wherever a culture was entering or was about to enter the era of writing. Such a system involves siting the capital city at the intersection of capital points and constructing a code of correspondences which gradually assimilates all creation within its system.[17]

Ultimately, a situation of absolute continuity between human microcosm and natural macrocosm is created.

MAGIC AND SCIENCE FACING TIME

If, as noted, the ritual is the actual repetition of the mythical event—it *is* this primordial event—then every ritual turns out to be, in a broad sense, a magical ritual. Magic in the strict sense is therefore only a specialized series of rituals, aimed at reconstituting the order and regularity of the world unsettled by some infringement of the rituals, or at propitiating such regularity in favour of specific individual and collective demands. Fundamentally, it thus intervenes in situations of discordance and discrepancy between the human and universal orders, as a specialized rite that abolishes them.

This specialization tends to render magic autonomous from its mythical-ritual context, that is, to transform it from an 'unavoidable technical moment' of this context into an independent technique.[18]

Here we are confronted with the complex problem of the relationships between magic and science. Suffice it to recall that, in this field, we are by now very far from the hasty condemnation of the former in the name of the latter. Magic provides humans with a precise mental and pragmatic method in situations of precariousness and danger, and contributes to the organization of social labour. It is therefore similar to science.[19] According to a more recent formulation, magic stands out as an articulated system of classification,

17 Leroi-Gourhan, *Gesture and Speech*, p. 329.

18 Ernesto De Martino, *Morte e pianto rituale. Dal lamento funebre antico al pianto di Maria* [Death and Ritual Lament] (Turin: Bollati Boringhieri, 1977), p. 40.

19 Malinowski, 'Myth in Primitive Psychology', p. 116.

capable of constructing a science of the concrete that, unlike science itself, does not operate with concepts but with signifying signs and images, by means of analogies and juxtapositions. Hence magic is not a 'timid and stuttering form of science'; instead, it is 'a sort of metaphorical expression of the latter' which differs from it especially with regard to the phenomena to which it applies.[20]

However, it is not only the difference in the procedures and phenomena under consideration that distinguishes magic from science but, rather, their final goals. Magic intends to reinstate an order that was perturbed, and its intervention on time is aimed at a *reconstitution* of the cosmic and human *cycle* at those points where it was interrupted. Science, on the other hand, is an integral part of a different project which, as we saw, is animated by a logic of exploration and conquest, as such antithetical to the one archaic people abide by. Its intervention on time, supported by incomparably superior technical means, thus goes in the direction of a *dissolution* of archaic cyclical time and the production of unprecedented temporal (and spatial) forms.

PROMETHEUS AND ANTI-PROMETHEUS

We have so far outlined some modalities of time annulment that, although sharing a common background, present differentiated characteristics.

The omnipotent annulment present in the child observed by Freud happens instantaneously, in the pure rhythm of the movement of the arm and the sound of the voice.[21]

In the archaic and periodic type of annulment, it is necessary to punctually comply with a mythical action; whence the central importance of the ritual, as a privileged modality to recreate the harmony between mankind and the universe.

The annulment we could call 'magical-technical' is unfolded through a series of specialized behaviours of growing complexity and laboriousness.

20 Lévi-Strauss, *The Savage Mind*, p. 13.

21 We should add that movement and sound are already the beginning of a magical *technique*, a physical-material procedure that functions as a support for the act of annulment. The sovereignty of the latter thus turns out to be diminished with respect to that permitted to dreams and fantasies.

What is the thread that links these different modalities and gradually causes the modification of our procedures with respect to time? The most immediate answer might be that experience *intervenes here, if we understand it as a collective accumulation, generation after generation, of cultural changes introduced by humans in the natural order and in the cultural order itself.*[22] *At a certain point, and in given circumstances, the variation caused by these molecular changes can no longer be counterbalanced, and overflows out of the circle of the repetition of the same on which archaic life is based. This gives rise to a time that is no longer ritually annullable but is instead accumulated indefinitely; this is what we usually call historical time.*

Yet we have to be clear about the way in which experience acts. It does not determine*—in a causal and mechanical manner—the passage to historical time. Rather, it* enables *the manifestation of something that is already implicit, as a resource, within the archaic world.*

22 I prefer the term 'experience' over 'history', which is more common in this field. 'Experience' is more neutral. Moreover, it is the accumulation of particular experiences, through countless generations, that *generates* history in the strict sense of the word. The term 'history' has increasingly been overloaded with a subtle ideological trap. It is not unusual to witness open attacks against 'history' by anthropologists and philosophers more or less explicitly bound to a metaphysics of self-identical Being. Remaining within the field closest to the present work, Mircea Eliade's *The Myth of the Eternal Return* is also an indictment against the destructive intervention of 'history' in the archaic world, so much so that, in the conclusion, we witness a surprising debate between an archaic and a historical man. The concretely historical motivations (persecution, war, etc.) that led the author to these conclusions and justify them are sufficiently clear, but this does not apply to the theoretical level. On the other hand, the term 'history' underwent an analogous reification—though opposite in valence—in the work of ethnologists and anthropologists of the 'historicist' orientation. For instance, in *Morte e pianto rituale*, De Martino's insistence on funeral rites as an operation of 'institutional de-historicization' (see, for instance, p. 347) and his open privileging of the historical world end up placing the entire matter of the ritual within the horizon of a 'pious fraud' (p. 281) that 'occults' the historicity of the various human operations (p. 283) as a 'technical mystification' (p. 353). With regard to archaic people, what follows is a (wholly 'historical') privileging of Christianity and the final glorification of the figure of the Mater Dolorosa (p. 336 ff.). In short, the very object of an otherwise rich investigation tends to disappear before the great sun of 'modern historicist awareness'. What always remains human as archaic is relegated to the status of disaggregated and outdated relics by 'historical becoming'.

This resource should therefore be fully visible within the archaic. Now, if the window from which we can look into the archaic world is provided by myths, then it is in them that we should recover this resource; and this is precisely what happens. In the Bible, man is originally in a garden of fruit trees 'nice to look at and good to eat'. But he really becomes what he is through a rivalry with God—that is to say, by eating the forbidden fruit of the tree of knowledge, which is God's tree. In Greek mythology too, the origins of humankind are strictly connected to the rivalry with God. In the beginning, human beings are similar to plants or animals; they are born from ash-trees and ants, or come out of the ground . . . Subsequently, we have the rivalry between Zeus and the Titan Prometheus; in order to help humankind, Prometheus steals the divine fire and gives it to humans. A celestial punishment follows: Prometheus is chained to a rock and exposed to an eagle; humans are condemned to the evils that Pandora has set free.

In these cases—to which others could be added[23]*—humans become humans by competing with God. It is the transgression of a prohibition or the appropriation of a divine asset that makes them overcome a purely biological condition. In myth, therefore, we already find the enunciation of the problem of a transgressive detachment from a superior order, which is at the same time a sin to atone for, and the proud and fearless inception of humankind as such. Prometheus is alive and active within a situation—the archaic one—that we could broadly define as anti-Promethean. We will later have to return to this dyadic situation* (see Chapter VII).

WHERE IS THE OBSESSIONAL?

We now need to understand the potential relationship between the obsessive procedure and these different modes of annulment.

23 This could be extended to the cycle of the 'trickster' of Native Americans. See, Paul Radin, Carl Gustav Jung and Károly Kerényi, *The Trickster: A Study in American Indian Mythology* (New York: Schocken Books, 1972). In this mythological cycle, we find a character that, according to Kerényi, encapsulates in himself the traits of both (the shrewd and cunning) Prometheus and his brother (the stupid and imprudent) Epimetheus, namely the two faces of a primordial human being (pp. 180–1). The trickster is possessed by an insatiable hunger and sexuality, yet also contains the 'promise of differentiation' (p. 168).

There is no doubt that, at first sight, the former presents a striking distinctiveness and peculiarity. The obsessional appears to be enclosed within his personal enigmatic endeavour, without any possible participation by others. And yet there is in his annulment something like a distorted echo of the other modes—the childlike-demiurgic, the archaic and the magical in the strict sense. This proximity seems especially noticeable with regard to the archaic annulment of a ritualistic kind.

The very word 'ritual' spontaneously recurs when we speak of both archaic people and obsessionals, prior to any scholarly specification. But the possibility of immediately grasping their similarity—the 'points of agreement' between the two, following the subtitle of Freud's *Totem and Taboo*: 'Some Points of Agreement between the Mental Lives of Savages and Neurotics'—is paralleled by that of seeing their extraordinary differences.

We said that, in archaic people, action is based on primordial models or premises, embodied in myths, from which they derive systems of rules and obedience. We can presume that, in the situations that are most significant for both the individual and the community, these rules assume the figure and duty of precise rituals. The infringement of these rules and rituals is given by an individual or collective action *devoid of a model*, which as such represents in the most precise way guiltiness or sin. At this point, various rituals of purification intervene, in which the recreation of the previously existing state of affairs—through the abolition of the time of sin—clearly prevails over a mere reparation.

In short, the time of myth is recreated in the time of acting according to rules; the time of infringement (that is, the time of non-legitimate experience) is removed through the annulment of time itself.

In the obsessional, the nexus between the infringement of rules, sin and purification through annulment is also evident. But this very nexus tends to be shapeless and to be caught up in an endless degradation. As we saw, the ritual or ceremonial loses vividness and is transformed into a variable series. Sin does not involve significant acts but their derisory simulacra; it is as if archaic civilization's code of universal correspondences were still in place but only in degraded and absolutely futile terms. Finally, the annulment goes through laborious and grotesque procedures.

Thus, on the basis of a personal problem, the obsessional seems to be driven to recreate a set of behaviours that manifested themselves as a unit in the archaic world. On this path, we could say that he tries to behave like an archaic man but, for reasons we will have to examine, fails to do so; he drags rituality *into modernity*, but from afar, in obscurity, through oblivion, and hence also with nostalgia (indeed one of the obsessionals I know explicitly speaks, at times with a sense of yearning, of a 'rhythmic punctuation of time' that actually *shows through* obsessions rather than dwelling in them).

What then is the reason for this search and concomitant failure? We have to turn to an element we have not treated so far, namely, the relation with mythical models.

III
THE FEROCITY OF THE ANCESTORS

THE DEAD AND THE ANCESTORS

Let us go back for a moment to the archaic humans facing their closest and most constant models, that is, what we somewhat hurriedly call their 'cult of the ancestors'—if this is at all possible, given that archaic humans have been historically exterminated or are rapidly withering away, and thus, by now, belong more to our imagination. The phrase 'cult of the ancestors' is for us reduced to an abstract and distant formula, one that we tend to read in the sense of a transparent and peaceful relationship between the living and the dead. And yet we should be suspicious about the profound subjection of living human beings to their forebears and progenitors; we should reflect on the (already repeatedly mentioned) fact that those who distanced themselves—even slightly—from past behaviours were immediately exposed to the most serious disasters.

In today's ordinary experience, most of us, Westerners, do not know any 'cult of the ancestors'; this social and historical distancing must have contributed to the fact that it easily appears to us in an ideal light, as something still and quiet. Undoubtedly, the numerous descriptions of ethnologists and mythologists are also responsible for this; it is easy to identify in them a *nostalgic* attitude towards the societies and forms of life they refer to, which is often combined with an unconcealed polemic against 'historical' society.

However, it seems to me that there is a stronger reason for such a common idealization of the 'cult of the ancestors', which often assumes a conservative undertone. That is to say, the fact that this 'cult' is often treated separately, if not independently, from the relationship archaic people have with their dead in a strict sense. Of course, everybody sees the passage from the dead to the ancestors, but this passage seems to happen in an obvious way, as if the dead *slipped away* and became ancestors.[1]

DEATH AND THE ARCHAIC GROUP

Now, all the available evidence concurs in pointing out the severity a case of death acquires within an archaic group, for both the close relatives and the whole group. But not every death is equally severe: the death of a foreigner, slave, weak or disabled person, child or woman has a minor impact and a different weight with respect to that of a full member of the group or a chief.[2]

Let us turn to a by-now classical description:

> Death among all the coastal natives of Eastern New Guinea causes a great and permanent disturbance in the equilibrium of tribal life. On the one hand, there is the stemming of the normal flow of economic consumption. On the other hand, an innumerable series of rites, ceremonies and festive

1 Ancestors seem to be missing only in some populations that follow an 'undifferentiated' or predatory economy (gatherers, hunters, fishermen—especially the last). In these cases, there would be with regard to the dead a simple distancing of a phobic kind (I will return to this). It is difficult to assess this data due to the almost universal interference of 'differentiated' levels. In any case, the transformation of the dead into ancestors seems to be linked, on the one hand, to the regularity of agricultural cycles and, on the other, to the prevailing importance of repetitive work over chance and adventure. As discussed, we are therefore within cyclical time, while in predatory situations 'man lives day-to-day, without projecting himself into the future; he does not master the temporal dimension and conceptualizes it with difficulty' (Jean Poirier, 'Problèmes d'ethnologie économique' in *Ethnologie générale*, Paris: Gallimard, 1968, p. 1608).

2 On these different degrees of severity, see for example Robert Hertz's classical study, 'A Contribution to the Study of the Collective Representation of Death' in *Death and the Right Hand* (Abingdon: Routledge, 2014), p. 76 ff. These are general considerations; they leave considerable scope for variations within each society; on a specific society, see Hélène Clastres and Jacques Lizot, 'La Part du feu. Rites et discours de la mort chez les Yanomami', *Libre* 3 (1978): 110.

> distributions, which one and all create all sorts of reciprocal obligations, take up the best part of the energy, attention and time of the natives for a period of a few months, or a couple of years according to the importance of the dead. The immense social and economic upheaval which occurs after each death is one of the most salient features of the culture of these natives, and one also which on its surface strikes us as enigmatic and which entices into all sorts of speculations and reflections.[3]

Malinowski's observations are corroborated by those of a more recent researcher, who worked in South America; for the Bororo people, 'whenever a native dies, an injury is done not only to those near to him, but to Society as a whole';[4] for the Nambikwara, 'death distinguishes men, on the one hand, and women and children, on the other. When the former die, they turn into jaguars, which consequently represent as many reincarnated humans. Instead, women and children disappear with the wind and hurricane, and they are not susceptible to any reappearance'.[5]

From this kind of remarks—which could go on for pages and pages—we can derive a general conclusion that, beyond the variety of statements, should be seen as inevitable:

> When a man dies, society loses in him much more than a unit; it is stricken in the very principle of its life, in the faith it has in itself [. . .] It seems that the entire community feels itself lost, or at least directly threatened by the presence of antagonistic forces: the very basis of its existence is shaken.[6]

3 Bronislaw Malinowski, *Argonauts of the Western Pacific: An Account of Native Enterprise and Adventure in the Archipelagoes of Melanesian New Guinea* (London: Routledge, 1999), p. 386.

4 Claude Lévi-Strauss, *Tristes Tropiques* (New York: Criterion Books, 1961), p. 219.

5 Claude Lévi-Strauss, 'La vie familiale et sociale des Indiens Nambikwara', *Journal de la société des Américanistes* 37 (1948): 1–132; here, p. 100. (See also *Tristes Tropiques*, p. 281.)

6 Hertz, 'Study of the Collective Representation of Death', p. 78.

Or, in terms that are essentially analogous:

> In a more general fashion this accounts for the paradox we encounter in primitive communities. Though in them the individual is of far less importance in himself than in more civilized ones, the death of an adult among primitives seems to be a far more notable occurrence, and it is the cause of far greater anxiety. This is because death, when it strikes, in reality deals a blow not at the individual, but, through him, at the group itself. The existence of the group is involved, and this is in danger.
>
> [. . .]
>
> When the head of the family or some other important member ceases to exist, the group in a certain sense begins to die also. For the real living being is the group: individuals exist only through it. Thus the group feels itself to be directly affected, for this death means the loss of some of its substance.[7]

THE DEPENDENCE OF THE GROUP

However, these considerations on the individuals who 'exist only through [the group]' may easily appear to be generic and exaggerated if we do not clarify what *kind of group* is here in question.

A group that is globally stricken in 'its substance' and 'the very principle of its life' when one of its important members dies—and thus all the more severely the greater the importance of the dead person—is undoubtedly a group that profoundly *depends* on this person. Whether we are dealing with a chief or the king of a tribe, a member of the counsel of the elders or, more simply, a father, this situation implies that the dependent group refers to him not only as

7 Lucien Lévy-Bruhl, *The 'Soul' of the Primitive* (London: George Allen & Unwin, 1971), p. 227. According to Georges Bataille, what society loses with every person who dies is not only one of its members but its own truth of permanence and continuity (quoted in Clastres and Lizot, 'La Part du feu', p. 110).

an established term of authority, power and prestige, but also as a *direct guarantor of its precarious survival.*

The following example is particularly incisive:

> Towards evening we had to come to a halt in the bush. We had been promised that there would be game thereabouts and the Indians, counting on our rifles, had brought no food with them. We, for our part, had brought only emergency rations which could not be shared out all round. A troop of deer which had been nibbling away at the edge of a spring fled at our approach. The next morning everybody was in a thoroughly bad humour: ostensibly, this took for its object the leader of the band, whom they considered to be responsible for the venture which he and I had devised between us. Instead of going off to hunt or collect wild food on their own account, they decided to spend the day lying in the shade, leaving it to the leader to find the solution to their problem. He went off, accompanied by one of his wives: towards evening we saw them coming back with their baskets heavy-laden with grasshoppers that they had spent the entire day in collecting. Grasshopper pie is not one of their favourite dishes, but the entire part fell on it, none the less, with relish. Good humour broke out on all sides, and on the next morning we got under way again.[8]

The narrator can thus conclude:

> Apart from one or two men who have no real authority, but are prepared to collaborate if paid to do so, the passivity of the band is in striking contrast to the dynamism of its leader. It is as if, having handed over to him certain advantages, they expect him to take entire charge of their interests and their security.[9]

8 Lévi-Strauss, *Tristes Tropiques*, pp. 287-88.

9 Lévi-Strauss, *Tristes Tropiques*, p. 305. See also 'La vie familiale et sociale des Indiens Nambikwara', p. 87.

In this situation, saying that individuals 'exist only through [the group]' means putting forward an abstract statement which leaves the door open for vacuous considerations on the annihilating power of the social Moloch (group, tribe, or society . . .). Instead, it seems appropriate to specify that a situation in which individuals profoundly depend on the group actually and inevitably entails a dependence on one or more people who embody that group. The group is always, explicitly or implicitly, hierarchized in a clear way; there are those who matter more and those who matter less or nothing; the majority of individuals can come to live their lives as if they were the property of the person, or persons, who embody the internal hierarchy of the group.

In other words, we can reach a state in which the majority of individuals genuinely *belong* to their chief or chiefs, and this is often corroborated by ethnographic observations. For example, in a study devoted to 'Kafir socialism', Dudley Kidd noticed that:

> among the Kafirs, the person of the individual belongs in theory to the chief: he is not his own, for he is the chief's man [. . .] The relation of the individual to the chief can be understood from the following statement made by a Zulu, describing to a white man the custom of the Festival of First Fruits. He said: 'The Zulus, if the mealies are ripe, are not permitted by themselves to eat them. The king must always give them permission before they do so. If somebody is eating new mealies, before the king has given his permission, he will be killed entirely. The white men are wondering about it, and say: "Is a man not allowed to go into his own garden for harvesting food, which he planted himself?" But the Zulus are not wondering about that, saying: "We are all the king's men: our bodies, our power, our food, and all that we have, is the king's property."'[10]

10 Quoted in Hans Kelsen, *Society and Nature: A Sociological Inquiry* (Chicago: University of Chicago Press, 1943), p. 18.

The individual belongs to the tribe chief to such a degree that one chief, called Shiluvane, issued in all seriousness the following decree: 'I do not allow of anybody dying in my country except on account of old age.' On the other hand, we should note that the Kafirs are allowed to hold private property and cattle; land cannot be sold or inherited; however, everybody knows that his lands will never be taken from him so long as he cultivates them.[11]

In this 'Kafir socialism' we thus encounter the literal realization of that belonging to a chief, or chiefs, that in the majority of other situations is not actually carried out. And yet, even in this case, individuals as such are not inexistent; unlike what some missionaries believed, we are not facing here the annihilation of 'the individual [. . .] the centralization principle pushed to its extreme, or to put it in another way, the death of all for the sake of one'.[12]

There is no 'overwhelming' submission but, more precisely, the sense of essentially belonging to the figure of a superhuman chief.[13] Although the outcome may appear to be roughly the same, it is nonetheless crucial to preserve the meaning of this distinction.

THE SPLITTING OF THE DEAD

In this context, it now seems clear why every case of significant death—that is, the death of full members of the group—arouses such great turmoil and vast reactions.

Initially, death is certainly the *experience of the dead*—of the body that does not move, the beloved who does not answer and the corpse

11 Kelsen, *Society and Nature*, pp. 18–19.

12 In Lucien Lévi-Bruhl, *Primitive Mentality* (London: Allen & Unwin, 1923), p. 401.

13 In the therapeutic groups studied by Wilfred Ruprecht Bion, the 'dependency group' is structured around the figure of a leader endowed with magical powers, from whom the group expects safety and protection and to whom, correlatively, it refuses an active collaboration (Wilfred Ruprecht Bion, *Experiences in Groups and Other Papers*, London: Tavistock, 1961, p. 146). This kind of behaviour immediately recalls that of the Nambikwara as described by Lévi-Strauss (see the previous point).

that decomposes.[14] But this experience does not suffice as such to account for the emotions that seize the group.[15] A sudden change of the internal structure of the group itself is required, and this change is linked with the rank of the dead; if the dead is the one who guarantees the survival of the group, his becoming a corpse *completely eliminates such a guarantee.* This entails two kinds of immediate effects.

The man who ensured the life of the group with his power is now suddenly reduced to the most radical impotence. The group that depended on his power is now immediately exposed to the risk of dying, of following the dead guarantor of its survival into nothingness. At this point, the situation becomes unbearable. The corpse does not move and the group is about to die. The only (forced) solution is denying death itself, as attested by that frightening immobility: *the dead man is not dead; he keeps on living.*

In this way, what emerges is the universal *splitting of the dead* (man-corpse and man-who-survives), that is, the universal belief in the survival of the dead whose necessity springs precisely from the position of immediate life-threatening danger the archaic group finds itself in when facing the death of its guarantor. *If the dead man does not die, then the group itself can continue to live.*[16]

14 Lévy-Bruhl has rightly insisted on this aspect, against any attempt to apply to 'primitives' the categories—typical of Western spiritualism—of 'soul' and 'body', and their related automatic separation at the moment of death: 'They have a name to designate him when he ceases to live here below, and has entered upon his post-mortal state. This name means "dead man", and there is no good reason for translating it "soul"' (*The 'Soul' of the Primitive*, p. 239).

15 See Hertz, 'Study of the Collective Representation of Death', p. 76: 'The horror inspired by the corpse does not spring from the simple observation of the changes that occur in the body. Proof that such a simplistic explanation is inadequate lies in the fact that in one and the same society the emotion aroused by death varies extremely in intensity according to the social status of the deceased, and may even in certain cases be entirely lacking. At the death of a chief, or of a man of high rank, a true panic sweeps over the group.'

16 Thus we can clarify what otherwise remains an unexplained and presupposed 'elementary fear of death', transferred to 'a concrete object, to the dead' (see Kelsen, *Society and Nature*, p. 214).

WE ARE OUR OWN ARCHAIC PEOPLE

The scene we described corresponds to an almost general answer which can be modified and specified within the different cultural configurations that ethnologists encounter. However, even in these general terms, it is not a fictitious example. Such a scene implies an experience each of us has lived or will live: the death of the beloved is always in part also our own death, and this is all the more true the more the dead person appears to be irreplaceable. In this case, their disappearance means the breakup of essential bonds, of relationships that are part of our own life—that are *this life—and an immediate anxiety about not being able to survive it.*

For this reason, fully spontaneous movements soon arise in us that, in their diversity and intensity, tend on the whole to deny and disavow the disappearance of that person, and make him live again before us. This happens by means of both memories and the relocation of the dead somewhere beyond *everyday life, a place that, however conceived, is initially the continuation in other—and very diverse—forms of his indispensable presence. What matters especially is denying that absence, the hopeless disappearance attested by the corpse.*

This impossibility of living the irremediable disappearance of the beloved, which is all the stronger the more this person is indispensable for us, is thus something we fully share with so-called archaic people; it does not divide us from them, although it is arguably more pressing in their case because their life is by far more precarious than the one we ordinarily experience. Facing death, facing certain deaths, we are ourselves internally our own archaic people, and—in a more or less forced way—continue to avail ourselves of a common process of denial. This entails the onset of a life based on the 'as if' *(as if that person were still alive) that can help us to survive, and overcome an otherwise unbearable moment, by compensating a void felt as immediately destructive with a new presence.*

From the outside, and from afar, it is no doubt easy to consider this new presence as an illusion*; but when we are gripped by the necessity that led us to deny that absence we are at the same time led to support our* beliefs *with all our strength.*

I deliberately used the terms illusion *and* beliefs*, since I think that the experience I described—shared by everybody—can legitimately be considered as one of the earliest moments of* religion*. Certainly, it is not the only one, but undoubtedly one of the most fundamental in the context of a religion typical of* *dependent human beings. But every religion has thus far been like that. It remains to be seen whether, as the theologian Dietrich Bonhoeffer claimed, we will reach such an extent of human 'independence' that a 'stop-gap' religion and god will no longer be needed.*[17] *This was also Freud's hope—albeit in a less optimistic way.*

CONSEQUENCES OF THE SPLITTING

This operation of death-denial nonetheless soon entails extraordinary vicissitudes, both individual and collective.

On the side of the dead person, if they continue to live, then their total exclusion from the relation with their family amounts for them not only to an extraordinary change but also an immense and objective *offence*, independently from the fate awaiting them in the afterlife. Moreover, the latter has never been imagined as actually preferable to concrete life—at least by the majority of humankind, otherwise the species would already have come to an end.[18]

What happens in the afterlife is therefore never an advantageous compensation with respect to the change and offence resulting from being dead. The attribution to the deceased of a series of reactions is derived from this fact; although such reactions are in relation with their previous personality, they are also largely similar to those of all other dead people: astonishment, feeling isolated and a desire for going back to the world of the living or dragging them to the grave, fury . . . Ultimately it is death itself—seen as an utmost degradation and at the same time as a passage to another life—that constitutes the basis on which the universal images of the offended and threatening dead—the one who restlessly comes back to the living—are established.

17 '[H]ow wrong it is to use God as a stop-gap for the incompleteness of our knowledge [. . .] We should find God in what we know, not in what we don't; not in outstanding problems, but in those we have already solved. This is true not only for the relation between Christianity and science, but also for wider human problems such as guilt, suffering and death. It is possible nowadays to find answers to these problems which leave God right out of the picture'—Dietrich Bonhoeffer, *Prisoner for God: Letter and Papers from Prison* (New York: Macmillan, 1959), p. 143.

18 Kelsen, *Society and Nature*, p. 53.

In turn, while the dead man is alive, offended and distressed, the group moves from total desperation for the disappearance of its lord to the anxiety associated with his anomalous and disquieting presence.

In the place of an absence, which is felt as lethal for the group, there is now an unpredictable presence, which runs the risk of being almost equally dangerous. It is therefore necessary to deal with it urgently.

DEATH AS MURDER

Now, the outcome of an examination of a vast range of ethnographic evidence is that death is interpreted according to two fundamental modalities.

First, death is a *crime*, a murder carried out by enemies through spells. In some cases, even natural death due to advanced age could not happen if there were no malefic interventions or if a beneficial intervention did not cease;[19] death in battle at the hands of another man is itself determined by somebody else, through the wounds inflicted by the enemy.[20] The following account by Strehlow is perhaps one of the best examples of such a way of conceiving death: among the Aranda

> every dead man is avenged, since all deaths are attributed to a foreign tribe and hence demand retribution. After the funeral ceremony the brother of the deceased addresses the assembled men: 'Tonight each of you will bring to the meeting a gururkna [a necklace or belt made of hairs of the dead] because tomorrow we shall go out and avenge his

19 Kelsen, *Society and Nature*, p. 97 ff.

20 Kelsen, *Society and Nature*, p. 4. After all we should not believe that such an approach, apparently very remote from us, is today completely absent. With regard to a member of the Red Brigades, who died in crossfire with the police, a newspaper reports the following (*La Repubblica*, 17–18 September 1978): 'Where did things go wrong—in the family, at school, in the factory? *Who should have intervened but failed to do so on time?*' (emphasis added).

death.' Thereupon they undertake an expedition of vengeance against some far-off settlement.[21]

There is no need to stress how uneconomic this solution is. If the expedition was actually carried out with the determination that transpires from the report, we should think that the existence of this veritable tribe of terror and vengeance must have caused serious problems to its neighbours.

In the context of this approach, various 'stratagems' were thus created which aim at obviating its most blatant setbacks; for example, the Batak replace the man that must be killed with a mere picture,[22] or the dead must settle for a fake punitive expedition instead of a real one: when the warriors come back home, nobody asks them whether they actually killed the culprit.[23] One should observe that, in these examples, the culprit is a stranger to the group; there is an important modification when the murderer becomes internal to the group. For instance, 'when several well-known men have died in an Ekoi village, suspicion is naturally aroused that they are the victims of black magic, and some friendless woman may be pounced upon as the probable culprit'.[24]

DEATH AS PUNISHMENT

This approach to death as the work of external agents (witches or sorcerers) is nonetheless less frequent than the second modality, according to which death is a *punishment* for the violation of taboos or traditional customs—and ultimately the *norms* of the group—as handed down by ancestors. In spite of the variety of situations, there are countless and converging examples of this way of conceiving

21 Kelsen, *Society and Nature*, p. 107.

22 Kelsen, *Society and Nature*, p. 102.

23 Lévy-Bruhl, *The 'Soul' of the Primitive*, pp. 228–9.

24 Kelsen, *Society and Nature*, p. 111. This situation corresponds to a first movement of internalization of death; through the scapegoat, the group begins to assimilate death.

death. Moreover, it should be stressed that, at times, the two approaches overlap, almost as if crime and punishment, victim and culprit, were not yet fully distinguished. This emerges in the following observation referring to the Warramunga tribe: 'It must be remembered that, though the man was declared by the old doctors to have died because he had violated tribal custom, at the same time he had of course been killed by someone, though by whom they could not yet exactly determine.'[25]

All in all, the most ordinary kind of death—the death we could rightly define as 'natural' for archaic people, which exempts the survivors from carrying out the onerous duty of revenge—is therefore the one of those who deliberately (or unwittingly, fortuitously or by means of magic trickery) violated the laws of the group. We could suggest that, should everybody follow faithfully the customs established by the ancestors, there would be a perfect and immortal community. And this is indeed what some archaic people claim: humans could live eternally if there were no evil spirits, influenced by hostile sorcerers, who avenge the offences that are inflicted upon the living or the dead—and these evil spirits are always souls of the deceased.[26] We will shortly return to this point.

DISTANCING

We now need to take a step back. Death is the last and final effect of a series whose first elements are illnesses and accidents. For archaic people, beyond a given threshold of seriousness, even these events clearly indicate a decision to sentence to death decreed by an offended authority, and thus involve an active process of self-defence by the group. Accidents, illnesses and death are events that expand

25 Kelsen, *Society and Nature*, p. 107. From the psychoanalytic standpoint, this situation is particularly significant: here we in fact witness to the inscription of death as guilt within a single individual; the previous persecutory setting is still present, although it is fading away and becoming less convincing.

26 Kelsen, *Society and Nature*, p. 99.

themselves and threaten to strike the entire group; from here follows the implementation of measures of radical *distancing*, which have so often offended and shocked civilized visitors.

As a paradigmatic case, I here report the clear description provided by John Liddiard Nicholas, who refers to an expedition to New Zealand at the beginning of the nineteenth century:

> No sooner does a person arrive at a certain stage of illness among them, than they believe the unhappy creature under the wrath of the *etua* [spirit]; and, incapable of accounting for the disease with which he is afflicted, as of applying a remedy to it, they can only consider it as a preternatural visitation of retributive justice, which it would be impious to resist by any human expedient. Many a poor sufferer who, with a little ordinary attention, might soon be restored to health and vigour, is devoted by this horrid superstition to perish in the very midst of his kindred, without a single effort being made for his recovery.
>
> [In the case of a chief who was dying for weeks,] they insisted that no human being should administer to his wants while he yet survived. The reason of their laying the poor fellow under this horrible interdict was because they now believed that the *etua* was fully determined to destroy him; and for this purpose had made a firm lodgement in his stomach, whence no mortal power durst venture to expel him, nor would he once quit his position, but remains there, increasing the agonies of the sufferer till he thought proper to put an end to his existence [. . .] Though the immediate family of Duaterra still continued to evince the same deep and tender affection as before, still they agreed with his other dependants in excluding him from any further assistance [. . .] And leaving him now entirely at the disposal of the *etua*, they were studious only about providing for his internment.[27]

27 Quoted in Lévy-Bruhl, *Primitive Mentality*, pp. 298–9.

THE OBLIGATIONS OF THE LIVING

Faced with a corpse, the group of survivors must initially scrutinize the death that occurred, assess guilt and responsibility and avenge—if death turns out to have been inflicted by enemies. Secondly, it needs to provide the dead with an honourable position in the unknown land he is traversing, one that is equally fruitful for him and the group *to which he continues to belong*, albeit according to different conditions.

Now, this task requires that the group reconnect with the corpse, even touching and handling it. As noted, the dead person indeed continues to live, because his life is the guarantee of the life of the group. Consequently, the group cannot keep him at a distance but must deal with him directly; if it did not, the group would be seeing one of its full members, or chief, devastated by his kin's extreme abandonment and at least in part endowed with the tremendous force of the dead.

Here the circle closes on itself. We said that death is generally caused by the transgression of the norms of the group which are watched over by the ancestors. Hence these dead people, who form the group's mythical heaven, directly or indirectly cause death. Therefore, the recently deceased—precisely and only insofar as they enter the afterlife—begin to partake of this celestial power over the life and death of human beings. At this stage, what reappears is the mortal danger for the group, which the creation of post-corporeal survival managed to avoid.

FUNERAL RITES, INCORPORATION, NORMS

From this follows the ubiquitous presence and essential function of funeral rites. The latter are absent only when the dead person has no rights and power in the group, and thus does not pose any fundamental problem with regard to life and death. As superfluous, inconvenient or alien to the group, he *really dies*, abandoned without fear or remorse in the bush or ravine outside the village. Here we encounter again, with respect to rites, that social difference in the outcome of death we already mentioned with respect to survival. Funeral rites are instead *owed* to those who have rights and power, under penalty of the most serious sanctions by the deceased or the ancestors for those survivors who do not comply with them.[28] If the rites are implemented correctly, they can establish the terms of an agreement between the deceased and the living.

In these archaic funeral rites we can distinguish two—at times entwined—phases through which the work of tribal mourning is carried out. The first is obviously prevalent right after death; the second can continue for a long period of time. A different *distance* of the dead from their group corresponds to this unfolding in two phases. According to many descriptions, initially, they wander restlessly, hungry for life or simply disoriented, next to their home and loved ones.[29] Subsequently, they distance themselves from them, yet without fully disappearing—at least for a long period of time.

The first phase essentially concerns the treatment of the corpse and the looming presence of the living dead. As noted, given that their death is, for the living dead, an impairment, isolation, offence, and in any case—even when deserved—a form of *violence*, every rite of this phase is intended to *appease* them as much as possible and thus free the group from their pervasive and threatening shadow. Very often, they are given food, drinks and shelter—in fact, they are in the curious position of being both dangerous and in need.

The second and fundamental phase goes beyond these operations of immediate urgency and satisfies the group's necessity to make the dead live so that the group is itself able to live.

28 This looming and threatening presence of the dead is what first and foremost distinguishes archaic funeral rites from those in force in current Western societies. While the former amount to a system of pressing obligations, to which the entire group is bound, the latter have substantially been reduced to ceremonials of affection or respect, which are often permeated by bureaucratic indifference. In this sense, they resemble the simple actions of distancing or cancellation of the dead that characterize the groups that follow a predatory economy (see note 1 on p. 36).

29 Lévy-Bruhl, *The 'Soul' of the Primitive*, p. 243.

It is therefore a matter of awarding the dead—in his new condition—with a kind of life that results into an assurance for the life of the group of which he is a member; ultimately, this is *a life in which there is no (longer) death.*

Now, a life without death is not and cannot be an individual life like the one we have always known. Through funeral rites, the individual dead must thus be absorbed into a trans-individual life, which, however, always remains in contact with the group; he becomes an *ancestor* and is included in the group of the ancestors endowed with a non-individual life, deathless and timeless.

But this is not enough: in the state of dependence in which the group finds itself, which at times even turns into a form of sheer belonging, it needs *the dead to live here*, now, among the living. The only way in which the group can obtain this is *by becoming itself the dead person*, becoming him in the living implementation of his attitudes and capacities. As properties of a being who passed away, the latter must become part of every member of the group.

In this respect, processes of *incorporation* of the dead are carried out by means of rites, and these processes entail at the same time the possibility of *repeating* the behaviours of the dead.

Incorporation always aims at an identification with the incorporated; we know that in the archaic group its modalities cover a wide range of similar or derived operations, such as cannibalism, consumption of the bones, symbolic ingestion and so on.[30]

It is clear that in this second phase of the elaboration of death by a dependent group we witness a twofold and parallel movement, namely, the eternalization of the dead person in the group of ancestors and his simultaneous incorporation by the group of the living. Through incorporation, the latter's behaviour tends to repeat that of the dead; and since the dead become eternal, their behaviours become the eternal *norms* of the group that has assumed them. The

30 See Hertz, 'Study of the Collective Representation of Death'; Clastres and Lizot, 'La Part du feu'.

group exits the radical crisis caused by death by means of a radical obedience to the norms of the dead. And this is the main reason for the 'steady state' of the entire group,[31] built upon the regularity of the occupations, ways of life and rituals of the ancestors—that is, upon cyclical time.

TRUCE, NOT PEACE

These are the final terms of the agreement. But it is important to stress that the latter repeatedly ratifies a truce instead of an actual peace. A situation that remains dangerous and tense is established; a minor deviation from the observance of rules suffices to unleash the fury of the offended forefathers.

Accidents (*disgrace* as the loss of the forefathers' protection and benevolence), illness and, again, death may thus follow. Rites of purification are being imposed with renewed urgency. If the precariousness of the life of archaic people is increased for whatever reason, then the relation of the living with the dominion of the living dead becomes anxious and darker, while the rites of observance and those of purification from infringements are intensified. The time of life—cyclical repetition—tends to turn into an exhausting and endless iteration. The relation becomes more domesticated and life breathes a sigh of relief only when this precariousness diminishes. In any case, this second eventuality is rarer and belated; in human vicissitudes, the good is always rarer and more belated than evil.[32]

We are therefore very far from the settled and pacified world described by some modern mythologists and critics.[33]

31 'The ordinary Balinese term for the period before the coming of the white man is "when the world was steady' (*doegas goemine enteg*)"—Gregory Bateson, 'Bali: The Value System of a Steady State' in *Steps to an Ecology of Mind: Collected Essays in Anthropology, Psychiatry, Evolution, and Epistemology* (Northvale NJ: Jason Aronson, 1987), p. 12.

32 Kelsen, *Society and Nature*, p. 60.

33 What strikes the reader even in Jean Baudrillard's *Symbolic Exchange and Death* (London: Sage, 1993) is the *immediacy* with which the archaic group would solve

The world is instead suspended in a precarious balance, continually exposed to destruction at the hands of the vengeful dead and laboriously rescued through observances and rites.

THE TIGHTROPE WALKER AND DESPAIR

The picture we have sketched so far, based on extensive evidence from various sources and periods, presents a quite clear common line. It seems to me that the obvious variables each individual archaic society can offer do not invalidate the basic outline.

However, one could detect almost a personal opinion in my final stressing of this world as 'on the edge' and in a precarious balance, which is opposed to the laudatory and even euphoric stance of many scholars. To answer this, I would like to refer to what a recent observer writes about a traditional society considered to be among the most peaceful and fortunate, namely, the Balinese: 'The rules are not of such a kind that they can be summarized either in a simple recipe or an emotional attitude. Etiquette cannot be deduced from some comprehensive statement about the other person's feelings or from respect for superiors. The details are too complex and too various for this, and so the individual Balinese is forever picking his way, like a tightrope walker, afraid at any moment lest he make some misstep.' This passage is followed by a list of the Balinese cultural contexts to which the metaphor of the tightrope walker is applicable, which first includes 'the fear of loss of support' as 'an important theme in Balinese childhood'.[34]

Moreover, an indirect confirmation of this precariousness is provided, quite unexpectedly, by the way in which some ethnologists characterize archaic rituals. At times, their description turns out substantially to overlap with that of an obsessive ritual. Suffice it here to mention Lévi-Strauss' stance as deducible from the

the relation between the living and the ancestors. As seen, this can be the case only if we overlook both the vast evidence we have on the tragic character of death in archaic groups and the set of rigorous operations on and with the dead that are necessary in every archaic group for the individual deceased person to be absorbed into the community of the ancestors. For Baudrillard, the almost exclusive key to the exchange between the living and the ancestors seems to be the 'rite of initiation' (see p. 131ff).

34 Bateson, 'Bali: The Value System of a Steady State', p. 128.

final volume of Mythologiques. *According to the French scholar, 'in all cases, ritual makes constant use of two procedures: parceling out and repetition'. With regard to the former, we are dealing with processes of differentiation and discrimination 'whose performance, through its infinite attention to detail, is carried to aberrant lengths, and gives the impression of "slow motion" camera-work marking time to the point of stagnation'. As for the latter, 'the same formula, or formulae similar in syntax or assonance, are repeated at short intervals, and are only operative, as it were, by the dozen; the same formula must be repeated a great many times running, or alternatively, a sentence containing a very slight meaning is sandwiched, and almost concealed, between accumulations of identical and meaningless formulae'.*[35] *In investigating the reasons for the systematic resort to these two 'complementary procedures' in the ritual—whose description could be transferred to obsessive ceremonials without changing one iota—Lévi-Strauss evokes a distinction introduced by Georges Dumézil with regard to archaic Roman religion. On the one hand, there is a small number of divinities constituted by oppositional triads or functional sets, whose reciprocal relation reconstitutes the global structure of the world and society; on the other, a plethora of minor divinities, assigned to the various—and meticulously separated—stages of this or that form of practical life (agriculture, cattle breeding, even childbirth). For Lévi-Strauss, these two categories of divinity—observable also in numerous other cults—correspond to movements of thought leaning in complementary directions; mythical thought, which splits the continuity of lived experience into vast distinctive unities (corresponding to Dumézil's major divinities), and the ritual, which 'takes upon itself the laborious task of patching up holes and stopping gaps, thus encouraging the illusion that it is possible to run counter to myth, and to move back from the discontinuous to the continuous. Its maniacal urge to discover the smallest constituents of units of lived experience by fragmentation and to multiply them by repetition, express the poignant need of a guarantee against any kind of break or interruption that may jeopardize the continuance of lived experience'. We therefore obtain an opposition between ritual and myth, corresponding to that between living and thinking, in which 'ritual represents a bastardization of thought, brought about by the constraints of life', a 'desperate, and inevitably unsuccessful, attempt to*

35 Claude Lévi-Strauss, *The Naked Man: Mythologiques*, VOL. 4 (Chicago: University of Chicago Press, 1990), pp. 672–3.

re-establish the continuity of lived experience, segmented through the schematism by which mythical speculation has replaced it';[36] *from this follows 'the characteristic mixture of stubbornness and ineffectiveness which explains the desperate, maniacal aspect of ritual'.*[37]

Lévi-Strauss' conclusion is therefore a radical belittlement of ritual with respect to myth; contrary to the former and like music or a certain historical form of music, the latter searches for and finds *a way out of difficulties, which is its precise theme.*[38] *Such a conclusion is evidently difficult to accept for those ethnologists who, observing certain concrete rituals, are at times compelled to acknowledge their success, precisely in the sense Lévi-Strauss denies. (On this, see the examination of the Ncwala—a regal ritual of the Swazi populations of Africa—carried out by a scholar who nonetheless explicitly refers to Lévi-Strauss' teaching.*[39]*)*

The question is evidently not that of opposing successful rituals to impotent and desperate ones but, rather, of understanding why in some cases the former are given, and in others the latter. This alternative is not only present in different societies but also within the same society and, we may say, even within individual rituals. From this derives the ambiguity that determines the extremely different interpretations among observers. See, for instance, still with regard to the Ncwala rite interpreted by Smith as a regal feat in the face of a cosmic threat, Max Gluckman's interpretation of it in terms of a 'rite of rebellion'.[40]

In my opinion, the key to solve this can only be found in the actual relation between myth (which is still, in its primordial moment, a mythical model*) and ritual. Using the distinctions introduced by Dumézil in a rather misleading way, Lévi-Strauss turns them into two opposite modalities of intervention in the real, doomed not to intersect. In the end, and in a very general sense, ritual is reduced to a secondary role, namely, trying to stitch up what myth sovereignly cut and disarticulated. Following this distinction, in an archaic society, a pacified relation*

36 Lévi-Strauss, *The Naked Man*, pp. 674–5.

37 Lévi-Strauss, *The Naked Man*, p. 679.

38 Lévi-Strauss, *The Naked Man*, p. 647 ff.

39 Smith, 'Aspects de l'organisation des rites', pp. 168–9.

40 Smith, 'Aspects de l'organisation des rites', pp. 157–8.

with myth and a 'desperate' and 'maniacal' relation with ritual could coexist at a given moment; such a ritual could subsequently be rightly referred to minor divinities, of an immediate practical order, while the major divinities—at least in the case where this differentiation is possible—would be deprived of a significant ritual organization. The opposite should hold for myths—as reserved to major divinities and removed from minor ones.[41]

We could instead more plausibly claim that the ritual is compelled to turn 'maniacal' and 'desperate'—or, more precisely, meticulous and insistent to the point of actual obsession—only where the relationship between those who carry out the ritual and the mythical horizon in which they intervene has become problematic and arduous. The despair of ritual is not isolated; it is born out of the crisis of the relationship with myth. In other—more familiar—terms, religion as an organized set of ritual acts turns *obsessive not because it is such from the outset (as Freud believed, at least at some point,*[42] *and as Lévi-Strauss still believes, moving from different presuppositions) but because the relationship with the worshipped god is in crisis.*

In this way Lévi-Strauss' description of rituals is therefore valid in two senses: as proof of the precariousness of the archaic world of which we have spoken, and as an indirect indication of the crisis of the relationship with the mythical models that underlies it. We are again in the field of that difficult truce with the ancestors, with regard to whom one needs to move like an acrobat on the tightrope. This is also valid, in completely different situations, for the obsessionals.

41 This is what Lévi-Strauss puts forward, to be honest, in a cautious way: 'Now, only the major divinities can be directly related to the myths' (*The Naked Man*, p. 674).

42 This is the stage corresponding to 'Obsessive Actions and Religious Practices', written in 1907 (*SE*, VOL. 9, 1906–1908). Subsequently, and especially in the 1927 *The Future of an Illusion* (*SE*, VOL. 21, 1927–1931), Freud outlines a more complex approach.

IV
THE OBSESSIVE LATH

A WORLD WITHIN ANOTHER

Many psychiatric and psychological treatises maintain that the obsessional is 'rigid'—that he has a 'rigid' personality. In my first contact with an obsessional, I instead quite often had the impression of a general attitude that tends towards the irreprehensible and irreproachable. Appearance must be impeccable, gestures essential, words measured and precise. Logical efficiency—or the adjustment of details—is often striking. Courteous docility and a subtle readiness to adapt to the interlocutor are also often evident.

At the same time, it all seems disembodied. It is all meant to avoid contact, the unexpected, conflict, the encounter. It is as though one is facing a pure mind offering to the external world a visible surface that is smooth, continuous and intangible. And yet this mind cautiously explores things; it studies secondary yet significant details and accumulates materials for later. Its requests are imperceptible but present.

Only some relatives, or some psychotherapists, are allowed to go beyond this surface—not always and not thoroughly. At that point, we see with amazement two radically different worlds coexisting, side by side, or better, one within the other. The first, which is in a subordinate position, moves according to rules that are for us recognizable and familiar; the second, which tends to prevail, imperiously functions according to procedures and apparatuses that strike us more because of a sort of separate logic than due to their strangeness. There is here an abstract and intellectual ruthlessness, almost as if the heat of the living organism converted into the schemes and articulations of an automatic device. Thus, when we are given permission, we find again in every obsessional what we observed in the man who annulled time, although in less developed forms.

However, it is crucial to stress that the obsessional is always in *both* worlds. For diagnostic purposes, textbooks insist on the fact that the obsessional is able to 'criticize' his obsessions. Of course, there is always an ability, however reduced, to look at and assess the work of the obsessive machine; at the same time, there is also always, to a different extent, a participation in it, something that goes far beyond formal rejection as well as the secret and shameful complicity with its operations. At any time, the obsessional is a bipolar structure, independently of the pole that is prevalent at a given moment. Participation therefore means, in a very clear-cut sense, being *part of* or having a *part in*. As enigmatic as he is to himself, the obsessional is at the same time also the creator of his own enigmatic nature.

THE OBSESSIVE POSTULATE

In order to clarify the genesis of this extremely singular situation, we are therefore compelled to put forward a postulate about the original position from which the obsessional phenomenology will later develop. Starting from the first year of life, there is a persistent *relationship of partial belonging* between the subject who will become obsessive and those who take care of him.[1] This relationship is characterized by the fact that the distinction between the two poles that constitute it—the child and the adult—has already taken place but *is not completed*; the borders between the two figures are still partially undecided. There is a link of reciprocal communication that presents, on the one hand, a weak, fragile and unsteady being and, on the other, a figure the child very much needs and depends on,

1 'Those who take care of him': the definition is intentionally generic, not only because it is not always the mother who takes care of the child, but also because psychoanalytic experience seems to point at more persons, who may also be (con)fused. See note 8 on p. 63 about the fantasy of the 'phallic woman'.

endowed in his eyes with traits of omnipotence. Insofar as he still belongs to that figure, the child participates in its omnipotence.

Adopting Margaret Mahler's model, we could say that there persists a stage of individual development that is intermediate between the symbiotic unity that joins child and mother and their complete separation into distinct unities; this is the so-called stage of differentiation.[2] We could also say that what intervenes is an arrested development in the transitional phase posited by Winnicott.[3] But rather than attempting to establish a precise moment of arrest within a development by stages, it is important to highlight the formation of a bipolar position, such that it hinders the subsequent development and thereby damages the child's process of autonomy.

The child hits a specific obstacle: every time he tries to separate he perceives his attempt as a destructive attack against the relationship with the adult who, due to his weakness, appears to him as the sole guarantee of survival. If he were less dependent, his separation would seem possible to him, if more or less strenuous, and he could accept the new distance from the figure he belongs to. Instead, in his case, every movement of separation and autonomy is accompanied by unbearable anxieties concerning the destruction of the other and, correlatively, of himself.

AUTONOMY AND THE DEATH OF THE OTHER

One wonders why this is the case. The first explanation is that the thrust towards autonomy in a being that (partially) belongs to

2 Margaret Mahler, 'On the First Three Subphases of the Separation-Individuation Process', *International Journal of Psycho-Analysis* 53 (1972): 333–8. For a critique of Mahler's approach, considered as adultomorphic and hardly consistent with facts, see Emanuel Peterfreund, 'Some Critical Comments on Psychoanalytic Conceptualizations of Infancy', *International Journal of Psycho-Analysis* 59 (1978): 427–41.

3 Donald Woods Winnicott, 'Transitional Objects and Transitional Phenomena: A Study of the First not-me Possession', *International Journal of Psycho-Analysis* 34 (1953): 88–97.

another implies as such, ipso facto, a violent act, a genuine fracture. It is not necessary to postulate any particular exacerbation—whether innate or acquired—of aggressiveness. On the contrary, we could claim that aggressiveness—understood at this stage especially as a thrust towards self-affirmation—is here particularly insufficient, given that the child has remained fixed to the relationship of belonging, that is to say, a relationship of passive safety and of delegation of responsibility. In these conditions, the thrust towards autonomy truly entails a traumatic event, something that sounds like a real death threat.

But perhaps such a thrust does not suffice to clarify the fact that the death threat primarily concerns the other. For Freud, at the origin of obsessional neurosis there is a desire for the death of the other, which is subsequently replaced by anxiety about the individual's own death.[4] We are here in the field of a sequence of events that is purely based on drives, which at most refers to a constitutional and organic determination of the drives themselves. Instead, the postulate I indicated essentially brings us back to the idea of a constitutive *network*, an interpersonal network of relations and desires.[5]

Now, insofar as the weak being is actually the child, his movement of separation should—in the first place or prevalently—entail an anxiety of self-destruction instead of the destruction of the other.

We could put forward the following hypothesis. In order to initiate the process of separation, the child must here rely on his own *identification with the omnipotent figure* to a degree far above average. Precisely because it is part of that figure, the child turns into it—and becomes an omnipotent figure—in order to separate from it. But in this exchange of roles, the previous persecutory anxieties—linked to the fear of losing this omnipotent figure—come to be triggered.

4 See especially Sigmund Freud, *Totem and Taboo: Some Points of Agreement between the Mental Lives of Savages and Neurotics* in *SE*, VOL. 13 (1913–1914), p. 59 ff / *GW*, VOL. 9, pp. 89–90.

5 Elvio Fachinelli, *Il bambino dalle uova d'oro* [The Child of the Golden Eggs] (Milan: Feltrinelli, 1974), p. 217.

In fact, in the basic situation we postulated, every interruption of the relationship on the part of those who take care of the child determines the emergence of violent aggressiveness, which, projected onto the adult, becomes a dread for the latter's aggressiveness. Abandoning the child even just for a moment, the adult is transformed into his active persecutor. Now, when in order to separate himself the child assumes the figure of the adult, it simultaneously becomes the persecutor of the adult-child. This is how the movement of autonomy is regularly accompanied by the appearance of anxieties relating to the death *of the other*.

THE POSITION OF UNDECIDABILITY

Eventually, a *position of undecidability* arises, an aporia with no possible solution. Remaining in the situation of belonging we delineated means having an identity, albeit one that is only sketched out, correlated with and dependent on that of the omnipotent figure. Precisely because of this weakness, the danger—and temptation—of a reabsorption in the previous fusional position is constant. Attempting to leave this position in order to create one's own independent identity involves the risk of destroying the relationship with the omnipotent figure and thus the emergence of a situation of isolation and guilty solitude, along with an immediate danger of annihilation. The position of belonging to and participating in the omnipotent pole of the dyad thus amounts to a lath suspended over two antithetical abysses: total compliance with the adult figure, which entails the disappearance of the self, and total autonomy from it, which involves an analogous immediate danger.[6]

6 At this stage, the obsessional seems to embody the situation that, in the history of Scholastic philosophy, is well-known as the paradox of Buridan's ass: placed midway between two identical piles of hay, it dies of hunger because it is unable to choose between the two. In Dante (*Paradise*, IV, 1–6), the analogy is even more compelling: in addition to speaking of 'two foods, equally removed and tempting' Dante also hints at a 'lamb standing motionless between the cravings of two savage wolves, in fear of both'. That is to say, he describes the situation of an individual

Suspended on this lath, the child stays still, and in this way it is only touched, *not pervaded*, by the anxieties caused by any movement. If in fact a shift towards a more intimate fusion with the omnipotent figure prevails, there soon arises the problem of the loss of his own identity, which, however limited and dependent, is nonetheless well present. At this stage, typical anxieties of child annulment are formed and the foundations are laid for the future frameworks of 'depersonalization'. If the movement continues, there appear persecutory anxieties in the strict sense; the subject's aggressiveness, unleashed by the enhanced pervasiveness of the adult figure, turns into the feeling of the latter's immediate aggressiveness, precisely because of the existing communication between the two poles of the relationship.

On the contrary, if the attempt to become autonomous prevails, then, as we saw, anxieties regarding the destruction of the other arise and an ensuing sense of guilt. Depression looms. If the sense of guilt is eroticized, then there follows the condition of 'psychic masochism' described by Edmund Bergler,[7] which is, however, a specific outcome of an ongoing process, and not a generalized one, as some scholars claim. Moreover, given that all this happens at a stage in which the oral relation is prevalent, such anxieties generally appear in every case as devouring anxieties—of devouring or being devoured.

To conclude, what thus constitutes the originality of this position is its being a point of balance—apparently precarious but ultimately

exposed to desires *or anxieties* that are equally balanced. There is not only a balance of appetites, but also one of *terrors*. It should be noticed that, according to the subtle Buridan, the (hypothetical) case of the ass does not apply to humans, since the latter are endowed with the *liberty of indifference*, that is, the possibility of arbitrarily choosing one or other solution. In this way humans overcome or suspend the judgement on the equality of goods (or evils) formulated by the intellect. It is noteworthy that, in the case of the obsessional, we are compelled to summon, at a certain point, even the difficulty or impossibility of assuming an autonomous, or 'arbitrary', choice.

7 Edmund Bergler, *La névrose de base* (Paris: Payot, 1963), especially pp. 26–9 and p. 32.

very solid—between psychosis and depression. Fundamental fantasies are elaborated around this point of balance and are obviously structured around the theme of the relationship with a hyper-powerful figure. We should therefore not be surprised by the frequency with which the fantasy of a relation with a phallic woman arises in the analysis of obsessionals, a phallic woman[8] with regard to whom the subject positions himself passively and at times masochistically. The vicissitudes of this image are parallel to those of his anxieties as a child. At times, the image is too invasive and fatally threatening; at other times, it is itself stricken by death.

A NOTE ON AMBIVALENCE

This particular immobility of the child standing on his obsessive lath tends to continue throughout the vicissitudes of development. One can find it again, in a particularly clear way, during the so-called sadistic-anal stage—which is, according to classical psychoanalysis, the fundamental, if not ultimate, end of regression in obsessional neurosis. It is from this point that those endless oscillations between activity and passivity, love and hatred, become particularly clear, which have led psychoanalysts to coin the rather vague and polyvalent term 'ambivalence'. But the regularity of anxieties and fantasies with an oral content compels us to go back beyond the anal stage, up to the period of separation-individuation. Furthermore, the postulate regarding the persistence of a relationship of belonging during this stage, which we delineated above, enables us effortlessly to unify the contradictory behaviours observed in the obsessional, which have indeed until now only been combined through the passe-partout notion of ambivalence.

8 For Freud, the 'woman with a penis' dates back to the child's disavowal of feminine castration. For Klein, this figure is constituted very early, as a figure of the mother that incorporates the paternal penis, and thus, in the end, the woman with a penis stands for the copulation of the parents. In the case of obsessionals, I have had several times the impression that what prevails in this figure is an aspect of pervasive terror, barely compensated by the human figure in which this terror is represented.

Even the problem of the obsessional's aggressiveness—which has been variously stressed or underestimated—finds a precise clarification in the undecidability of the dual relationship, instead of in the speculative presuppositions of an 'instinctual defusion'.

THE OBSESSIVE SOLUTION

As the child grows, internal and external solicitations aimed at leaving the state of dependence become more pressing. If at all possible, the child bound to the relationship of belonging often reacts by *changing the person* to whom he refers in this relationship, without modifying its fundamental characteristics. For example, it thus frequently happens that a relationship with the paternal figure or another relative is established which, to an external observer, can seem to be primary for a long time and of an importance that is absolutely incomparable with the relationship with the mother.

However, at a certain point, the real thrust to leave the orbit of the dual unity can no longer be eluded; around puberty the assumption of an independent identity becomes inevitable.

We often witness a stage of uncertainty, feeling empty, 'boredom', 'aboulia' and 'indolence'—these are all terms with which one designates (internally or externally) a situation that is grey, static and appears as a kind of wait. Soon thereafter, it is in fact replaced by the appearance of an *obsessive solution* in the strict sense. In a certain way, we could say that this is a new stratagem aimed at preserving at any price the relationship of belonging. If the latter is no longer sustainable by means of a change of person, it will be preserved by changing the *ground* on which it unfolds.

This is how it happens: through the participation in omnipotence that characterizes him, the subject carries out a *displacement* of the dilemma that afflicts him into a field that is different from the one we call real, that is to say, into a world of symbolic-magical *equivalences* and *correspondences* which is indeed opened up by omnipotence. The first step in this direction is often the creation of areas, beings or situations to be avoided and kept at a distance; these are the so-called phobias which are named in different ways according to the object or moment to which they refer. But other displacements soon follow.

In this way—and that is the 'advantage' of the operation, if we may say so—the relationship of omnipotent belonging is maintained, and its maintenance constitutes a safeguard from those persecutory and depressive anxieties that beset the subject. However, the price of this operation is a radical depersonalization of the dilemma, and of the very subject of the dilemma, in the direction of a paradoxical *socialization in a magical world.* Let us not be fooled by the secrecy and privacy of the acts that are being carried out: in becoming what he is, the obsessional has radically departed from his personal individuality.

The object of the dilemma—becoming oneself at the expense of the death of the privileged partner—changes and can be recognized only by means of associative and symbolic links. The concrete subject of the dilemma does not vanish from the scene, but he only appears on it with that lifeless and empty look we referred to earlier. Another enigmatic character materializes behind the obsessional and looms over him like a mountain. This is the partner who has been threatened with death and now radically changes his physiognomy. Already interiorized [*interiorizzato*] in a position of omnipotence—already put on the throne [*intronizzato*], we could also say—he now becomes a majestic authority, an inexorable law and a nameless rigour. In this way, a ruthless body of laws is constituted, a sinister and grotesque legislative monument: decrees and prohibitions, permitted and forbidden activities, lawfulness or unlawfulness, 'for' or 'against' an impersonal 'system'—the typical 'system' we indeed encountered at the beginning of this book. Before this system stands a vassal who, in order to save at least a minimal part of himself, *flees* towards what is insignificant and futile, towards an almost invisible periphery; he literally turns into dust under the feet of the power that chases him down.

THE DEADLOCK

But this is not enough to eliminate the terms of the original dilemma. While, thanks to the omnipotent equivalences, the dilemma becomes more distant and unrecognizable, at the same time and because of the same equivalences, it also remains untouched and unsolved, like at the outset. The obsessional wears himself out in the attempt to remove something that, through the ramifications of thought, returns to him like a boomerang. The dilemma is less dramatic—precisely insofar as it is displaced and hidden—but has an extraordinary oppressive force. The obsessional again faces the spectre of the death of the other; this is the continuous temptation to breach the 'system', insult God, contaminate and foul . . . This is once again the risk of injury and the disappearance, for which the obsessional is responsible, of the ultimate term of his primitive relationship of belonging. The fact that this term has changed and become unrecognizable does not matter; the 'offence' to the law, however bizarre and ridiculous they both seem, always expresses the original dilemma.

In the offensive act, whatever it is, one can read the persistent thrust towards an independent identity, and the 'offence' is really itself a prelude or realization of the destruction of the other. This is confirmed not only by the associative links we are in a position to establish but also by the immediate consequences that the 'offense' entails; that is to say, the surfacing of anxieties that, at times, coincide with the—literally devouring—ones of which we have spoken.

GUILT AS A RITE OF ATONEMENT

Notwithstanding the displacements they might undergo in the world of magical equivalences, the terms of the dilemma thus remain the same. The death threat addressed to the partner is omnipresent along with the problem of guilt. However, we must here highlight an essential aspect of this problem; insofar as the entire field of the dilemma, including its protagonists, is displaced onto an impersonal ground, the problem of guilt is itself presented in impersonal terms.

In place of a self-accusation accompanied by remorse and repentance, guilt is here a *rite of atonement*. This is another fundamental aspect of that paradoxical 'magical socialization' carried out by the obsessional. The so-called obsessive ceremonial is an attempt to endlessly bring deathless life to an authority that is indeed threatened with death. At this point, the very content of the ceremonial is never accidental, that is, the result of a free wandering in the infinite world of magical equivalences. In a direct or indirect way, through an explicit or allusive repetition, and always imperiously, the ceremonial has in every case to do with a moment of the actual historical exercise of authority with respect to the subject who subsequently became an obsessional. Let us consider one of the simplest cases, namely, the obsession with dirt and impurity; the ceremonial of cleansing, in its rigorousness, is always an exaltation and even an emphatic calling back to life of the gestures and orders originating from the authority in one of the *critical* moments (the so-called sadistic-anal stage) of the relationship with it—when the tendency towards one's autonomy clashed most heavily with the authority.

Ultimately, the machine-like mechanism that the obsessional sets magically in motion is compelled to legislate first and foremost on the acts and incidents of a childhood event.

THE (CON)FUSION WITH THE DEAD

But it is the entire universe of physical and mental relationships that may become the object of the attempted ceremonial regulation, precisely because each of them is not valid as such, as a 'natural' moment inscribed into a logic of stages or drives, but as a real term that took place as part of an unsolvable dilemma. Through the repetition of gestures and formulas, the obsessional glorifies the authority that he simultaneously threatens to destroy.

This is why, instead of being regularly punctuated according to well-defined intervals, the cultic time of the obsessional proves to be fatally interrupted by the intervention of a profane time, which profoundly disrupts it and, as we saw, at times makes it necessary to proceed with laborious procedures of annulment. This is also why the ceremonial in turn undoes itself and becomes an exhausting and endless repetition; the death of the other, whether threatened or executed, is always present and ineliminable. The obsessional is unable to distance himself from the dead, and at all times he repeats his killing and atonement for it. In this sense, his life—if we can call life that mechanical frenzy of death gestures accompanied by gestures of salvation—ends up being reduced to a mere *(con)fusion with the dead.* The relationship of omnipotent belonging is accomplished by sacrificing one's entire life to it.

V
AN ARCHAIC MICROSOCIETY

We can now try to summarize and enrich what we explained in the two previous chapters.

THE GOVERNMENT OF THE LIVING-DEAD

Facing a phenomenon that exceeds common abilities to comprehend and control, the archaic group generally adopts an elementary measure of self-defence which consists in *distancing* and physical separation. We saw how even facing a case of death, the group often tends to repeat this kind of measure. But precisely in the case of death, the latter immediately turns out to be insufficient.

In fact, the death of a member of the group strikes it *in its totality*, in a way that is proportional to the importance and rank of the dead person in the group itself (this proportionality, which is intuitively evident, should be understood in a very general sense). From this and other anthropological observations we inferred that the group is in a position of *dependence-belonging* with respect to its most important *value-figures*, to the extent that their death is felt as a catastrophe that can drag the entire group down with it.

Separating from the corpse is therefore not enough; something far more radical is needed. This radical way out is given by the *denial of death* itself, a process that lies at the basis of the universal belief in the survival of the dead. At this point, the group again approaches the corpse and engages in a series of various and complex procedures which are, in general, strictly codified and constitute as a whole the *institutions of mourning*.

These procedures usually have two stages: the first is devoted to appeasing the restlessness of the living and the dead; the second establishes a relationship of truce, if not actual peace, between them. These procedures always come to an end with the insertion or reabsorption of the individualized dead into the community of *ancestors*—whatever name may be given to the latter.

At this point the archaic group, which has eliminated death, has a bipolar structure: on the one hand, we find the group of the living in the strict sense; on the other, the community of the living-ancestors. The relationship between these two poles of the group is extremely close. On the basis of the complex vicissitudes we have presented, the living-ancestors *support* the behaviours of individuals and the whole group of the living according to customs that are in general rather rigid and whose infringement often entails the punishment and death of the transgressor, if not of the whole group. This is the inflexible government of the living-dead.

The fundamental elements on the basis of which the archaic economy of death is constituted are thus the following: a state of substantial dependence on the value-figures of the group; the denial of death; the formation of the community of ancestors.

THE OBSESSIVE LAW

At the origins of obsession, we postulated a situation of partial belonging of the child to the figure of omnipotence. As soon as the actual obsessive framework is constituted, we are faced with a very close relationship between the concrete and living subject on the one hand, and an internal pole of magical omnipotence—the obsessive Law—that dominates him on the other.

The point of passage between these two situations is constituted by a dilemma which involves a problem concerning death. Due to his relationship of belonging, the subject lives his aspirations as a mortal danger or a putting to death of the privileged partner—which conversely means putting oneself to death. Analogous problems arise from *renouncing* these aspirations.

In the impossibility of overcoming the dilemma, the obsessional carries out a displacement which may at first look like a simple distancing, whether spatial or not (we are at this point facing a determinate *phobia*), but which often, in a short time and because of the insufficiency of this measure, becomes an actual transposition of the relationship onto a generalized magical level. In this way, the original dilemma along with the dangers it entails is often concealed, if not erased; but it also surfaces as untouched within every subsequent displacement.

IDENTITY OF MOVEMENTS AND DIFFERENCES OF OUTCOME

This brief summary makes it clear that the fundamental movements that constitute the community of ancestors for archaic people on the one hand, and the Law or rigorous Norm for the obsessionals on the other, are the *same*.

The outcome is the formation of a pole of magical control that supports the behaviours of the group in one case, and that of the obsessive individual in the other.

However, having posited this identity of movements, it does not at all follow that the archaic group can be defined as obsessive or that the obsessional is upon closer inspection archaic.

We saw that among archaic people those who transgress die and, vice versa, those who die transgressed; in the obsessional, the transgressor cannot die, because he is vitally united with the devout in the same person.

This alters the whole process of the reabsorption of the guilty dead into the impersonal universe of norms. If the transgressor does not die, and is always active (although, at times, in a very reduced way), then the punishment is never really fulfilled and must be reiterated. Hence, in principle, the ceremonial corresponding to the archaic funeral rite that gives access to the universe of norms cannot itself be concluded. The former actually turns out to be even more unbearable than the latter, which nonetheless contains clear elements of threat.

Transgression, punishment and reparation are always present together, at all times.

What follows from this is the typically obsessive *whirlpool* or *ring-around-the-rosy*,[9] namely, that dancing around the same point, without a real change of position, that characterizes obsessive vis-à-vis archaic behaviour—in spite of the identity of the moments it consists of.

THE OBSESSIONAL AS AN ARCHAIC MICROSOCIETY

This is where the difference lies.

In the archaic group, transgression is concentrated in an individual who is sentenced to death; he is separated (in his death-guilt) from the rest of the group, which, albeit in dramatic conditions, manages to purify itself and the dead, reabsorbing him into the world of the ancestors.

In the obsessional, the transgressor cannot be isolated and punished, and this fact therefore gives rise to a continuous activity of purification. The process of mourning cannot be accomplished and therefore needs to be repeated infinitely.

In the end, the obsessional is a micro-group, an archaic microsociety in which one of the fundamental operations of the economy of death has failed.

TOTEM AND TABOO: THE CONSTRUCTION OF A JIGSAW PUZZLE

At this point, it seems necessary to compare the data we have obtained with that of the most significant precedent in this field of research, namely, Freud's *Totem and Taboo*.

All the numerous threads that run through the book (totemism, exogamy, taboo, children's phobias, animism, magic and so on) tend towards the same goal, that is, the construction of the 'monstrous' hypothesis about the sons who kill the tyrannical primordial father

9 'Ring-around-the-rosy' [*girotondo*] is the definition an obsessional quoted by Gilda De Simone Gaburri gives to characterize his own life (see *Il tempo e la relazione analitica* [Time and the Analytical Relationship], unpublished manuscript, 1979).

and devour him, thus putting an end to the paternal horde and commencing 'so many things—[. . .] social organization, [. . .] moral restrictions and [. . .] religion'.[10]

As is clear from the text, this final hypothesis is established through the juxtaposition of some preliminary elements which are made to fit with one another like pieces of a jigsaw puzzle.

Let us briefly hint at them. First, there is Darwin's idea of a primordial horde dominated by the strongest male, who keeps all the females for himself and drives the younger males out. In this way exogamy is imposed on the latter.[11] Second, there is the evidence of animal phobias in children; they are interpreted as a displacement onto animals of the child's ambivalent feelings for the father. In this way, children's phobias mark a 'return of totemism'; in fact, if the animal is the father, then 'the two principal ordinances of totemism, the two taboo prohibitions which constitute its core—not to kill the totem and not to have sexual relations with a woman of the same totem—coincide in their content with the two crimes of Oedipus, who killed his father and married his mother, as well as with the two primal wishes of children'.[12]

At this point, Freud adds William Robertson Smith's hypothesis about a 'totem meal', that is, a feast during which the totemic animal of the group—the divine animal—would be killed and eaten in order to reinvigorate the bonds of the group through its sacrifice and shared consumption.[13]

By connecting these three elements, Freud constructs his hypothesis about a rebellion in the horde against the tyrannical patriarch, the sons' murder and eating of the father. This is essentially also James Jasper Atkinson's hypothesis. Through the sons' sense of guilt, Freud complements Atkinson with the institution of the fundamental

10 Freud, *Totem and Taboo*, *SE*, VOL. 13, p. 142 / *GW*, VOL. 9, pp. 171–2.

11 Freud, *Totem and Taboo*, *SE*, VOL. 13, pp. 125–6 / *GW*, VOL. 9, pp. 152–3.

12 Freud, *Totem and Taboo*, *SE*, VOL. 13, pp. 126–32 / *GW*, VOL. 9, pp. 154–60.

13 Freud, *Totem and Taboo*, *SE*, VOL. 13, pp. 132–40 / *GW*, VOL. 9, pp. 160–9.

taboos of totemic religion as well as the foundations of society and morality.[14]

Freud's construction is therefore based on two hypotheses (Darwin's primordial horde and Robertson Smith's totem meal) in addition to data pertaining to psychoanalysis. It is easy to see that, should the two preliminary—and broadly speaking anthropological—hypotheses collapse, the only support for the Freudian framework would indeed be that data which is alien to the anthropological field. We are thus dealing with a suggestive yet extremely fragile construction whose fall runs the risk of dragging the entire book down, since it is clearly aimed at its enunciation.

This is indeed what happened historically. The ethnologists' refusal of the Freudian 'myth' of origins turned into a discrediting of the whole work.

Totem and Taboo: The Problem of 'Agreements'

However, the basic question from which Freud's investigation moves was in this way underestimated; that is to say, the existence of similarities, surprising coincidences or 'agreements between the mental lives of savages and neurotics', which are striking though they remain enigmatic. This is the important point that ethnologists generally rejected—with the exception of those who followed Freud's lead more or less closely. They were entitled to do so: after all, the problem of obsessional neurosis did not concern them, at least at first sight. But I believe that their refusal also contributed to limiting psychoanalytical research on obsession to a technical field, where it can only find partial solutions.

Let us reconsider these 'agreements'. Some of them—such as that between children's animal phobias on the one hand, and the relation with the totem on the other—turn out, upon closer inspection, to be highly speculative; they presuppose the acceptance of a

14 Freud, *Totem and Taboo*, *SE*, VOL. 13, p. 140 ff. / *GW*, VOL. 9, p. 172 ff.

series of additional interpretations which only some psychologists or anthropologists are ready to acknowledge.

However, there is still the problem of a specific individual situation—obsessional neurosis—in which we can detect a series of absolutely peculiar phenomena that are at the same time, at first sight, quite similar to those observed in archaic societies (taboos, ceremonials, magic). What should we make of them?

Following Freud's interpretation step by step one can see that it is substantially identical in both cases except for a particular point.

For example, in the case of *taboos* on the one hand, and *obsessive prohibitions* on the other, Freud observes that they are mysterious with regard to their origin, extremely mobile (they extend from an object to another following every trace of a connection), contagious, irreversibly sustained and the source of ceremonials.

On the level of phenomenal appearance, we are thus facing a perfect coincidence. Even with regard to their formation, we are dealing with an identity: according to Freud, taboos and prohibitions in fact emerge as a consequence of a forbidden action towards which there is at the same time a strong inclination. This inclination is repressed in the unconscious and there thus arises a lasting situation of ambivalence; given that the forbidden inclination moves continuously, in order to elude the barrier it encounters, the prohibition is itself displaced. At this point ritual practices of purification emerge, in which it is also easy to read the fulfilment of the forbidden action.[15]

Totem and Taboo: What Is Forbidden?

According to Freud, the only point where obsessionals and primitives diverge is in the *type of forbidden action.*

While for obsessionals what is at stake is touching one's genitals, that is, masturbation,[16] in the case of primitives it is a matter of

15 Freud, *Totem and Taboo*, *SE*, VOL. 13, p. 29 ff. / *GW*, VOL. 9, p. 38 ff.

16 Freud, *Totem and Taboo*, *SE*, VOL. 13, p. 29 / *GW*, VOL. 9, p. 38.

sexual relations with members of the same totem and the killing of the totem animal. In the case of primitives, the forbidden contact would therefore have a different meaning from the obsessional's masturbatory one, namely, the 'more general sense of attacking, of getting control, and of asserting oneself'.[17] This preponderance of the sexual drive components over the social ones would be what characterizes neurosis, turning it into an asocial formation.[18]

However, we can now observe that this distinction fades away not only in Freud's subsequent investigations, when the 'social drives' are abandoned, but also, for the most part, in the course of *Totem and Taboo* itself. Indeed, Freud repeatedly claims that the presence of the desire for death and aggressiveness is also fundamental to obsessional neurosis. While in primitives this desire is projected outwards—hence it is the other, the unconsciously hated person who becomes hostile for the subject—in obsessionals it gives rise to self-accusations or turns into an anxiety for the death of the other, yet it always remains easily recognizable.[19]

At this stage the specific difference, that is, the asocial character of neurosis is exclusively founded on the type of forbidden contact.

Here we should ask: what is prohibited in masturbation? Or better: in what way does the prohibition affect the masturbating child? On the basis of ordinary experience, as well as the findings of psychoanalysis, it seems we can suggest that he is affected not only, and perhaps not so much, in what concerns the sexual activity carried out through masturbation, but also and especially with regard to the 'self-assertion' that the former inevitably entails. It is a manifestation of independence, autonomy and self-sufficiency; and these are precisely the aspects that are first and foremost targeted in masturbation. Hence, from this stance too, there is no clear distinction between obsessional neurosis and archaic people.

17 Freud, *Totem and Taboo*, *SE*, VOL. 13, p. 73; see also pp. 33–4 / *GW*, VOL. 9, pp. 90–1, p. 44.

18 Freud, *Totem and Taboo*, *SE*, VOL. 13, p. 73 / *GW*, VOL. 9, p. 91.

19 Freud, *Totem and Taboo*, *SE*, VOL. 13, in particular p. 61 ff. / *GW*, VOL. 9, p. 76 ff.

In both cases, what is at stake is something 'more general' that has to do—obviously on very different levels—with mastery and self-assertion, along with their prohibition. And yet the fact remains that these terms are not interchangeable. The individual agreements established by Freud seem solid, but the final outcome is not at all identical. This cannot be due to a difference in the field of the drives at stake, as Freud himself believes—sexual drives in the case of neurosis, social drives in that of groups. As we saw, this kind of difference tends to disappear if we simply delve into the indications provided by Freud's text. Thus the difference in outcome can only be due to the fact that, in archaic groups, the process is articulated through the distinct positions occupied by individuals within a global collective, while in obsessionals it is unfolded within a single individual who assumes, so to speak, all the positions of the group. In the first case, the dead person has a clearly *separable* position with respect to the rest of the group; in the second, the dead person is permanently *co-present* within the individual. This is precisely what we can infer from our investigations.

A COMMON PROBLEM

In this way, obsession does not originate from an unexplainable and obscure constitutional archaism or from a hereditary repetition, in a Lamarckian sense, of archaic ways of life. Archaic people and obsessionals both confront, in totally different conditions, a common problem.

We can thus clarify the—very easily repressed—enigma about the behaviour of individuals in whom we are compelled to recognize ways of acting—however pronounced and exasperated—that belong to humans who lived countless generations ago, about whom these individuals often do not know anything.

And there is more to it. Just as these modalities can be presented again in individuals, so can we find them to be active in other groups and societies which are completely different. This is what we will now consider by way of a recent historical example.

VI
THE FASCIST PHENOMENON

'REVELATION' OR HISTORICAL 'PARENTHESIS'

When was Fascism born in Italy? According to a well-known hypothesis, Fascism was the ultimate and inevitable consequence of a series of deficiencies or faults in Italy's historical development, of which it would appear to be a resounding *revelation* in extremis. Today, this hypothesis has fallen into disrepute among historians, due to both its mediocrity and the frequent sectarianism of its contributions, as well as the criticisms that other scholars levied against it.[1]

Suffice it to recall here Federico Chabod's remarks, which follow those of Benedetto Croce:

> We can no longer claim that Fascism was a mere 'adventure' that suddenly intruded into Italian history, as if coming from outside. It seems to me equally beyond doubt that themes and attitudes in Italian life that had long been latent appeared in plain sight in Fascism, starting with the nationalist spirit—which was not purely an imitation of foreign matters, although it was fomented amid and by such foreign attitudes [. . .] But—and on this point Croce is absolutely right—these seeds did not *necessarily* entail Fascism [. . .] At the origins of Fascism—that is, during the crisis of the Italian ruling class between 1919 and 1922—some proclivities and attitudes that had indeed been present in the period

1 See Renzo De Felice, *Interpretations of Fascism* (Cambridge MA: Harvard University Press, 1977).

of 1870–1914, but only in a subordinate position, became decisive elements; but the turning of the *purely potential* and non-decisive elements into a decisive and actual political reality happened only at that point, at that precise moment, as a consequence of the sins and mistakes of those men, and not of those of 1860 or 1880 [. . .] It is then that the 'precedent' posed by nationalist attitudes, etc., could become elements of a strong and even decisive appeal; and yet, until the end this outcome was not 'inevitable' or predetermined [. . .] Therefore, it is all the more true that in the history of Italy from 1859 onwards there was nothing that 'inevitably' led to that outcome; similarly, those who study the history of Italy between 1860 and 1915 by projecting onto it, after the event and in hindsight, the shadow of 1922 and 1925, assessing it *only* in accordance with this shadow, go astray and are far from writing genuine history.[2]

As De Felice notes, Chabod's remarks conclusively clarify not only the hypothesis of *revelation* but also that of Fascism as a historical *parenthesis*, a period of 'moral sickness' separated and isolated from the rest of Italian history. The latter is Croce's well-known hypothesis:

When a man who is healthy and strong falls mortally ill, this is certainly because he had in himself the possibility of illness; and yet it was right to consider him as healthy and strong as a healthy and strong man can be, that is, as

2 Federico Chabod, 'Croce storico' [Croce as Historian], *Rivista storica italiana* (October–December 1952): 518 ff. These observations can be perfectly matched with what Golo Mann says about Germany: 'The failure of the Republic [of Weimar] proves nothing about the historical validity of what came after it and much too much honour is done Hitler by historians who want us to believe that all that Germany did for hundreds of years was to prepare itself for the inevitable end, for National Socialism. Particular ideas and sentiments which Hitler used, pan-German nationalism, imperialism, the desire to have a strong man, and anti-semitism, had of course long been there in the German soul, yet such ideas alone did not constitute an historically effective force'—Golo Mann, *The History of Germany since 1789* (New York: Praeger, 1968), pp. 416–17.

someone who is not immunized against the possible illnesses and epidemics that may occur.[3]

THE NOVELTY OF FASCISM: UNINTERPRETABLE FASCISM

Thus there were, prior to Fascism, 'seeds' of or a 'precedent' for it. But the difference in importance between the latter and actual Fascism was such that Fascism was perceived as something new, unheard of, and absolutely extraordinary for the life of the country. Croce's expression 'parenthesis' should be understood in this sense; certainly not in terms of an irrelevant series of events, which come and go without leaving a trace, but as a *way* of functioning of history itself, radically different from what had been known up to that point.

There was therefore no linear transition between the 'seeds' of Fascism and Fascism itself. Instead, due to an exceptional situation, these ineffective—or scarcely effective—seeds assumed an exceptional power. Historians unanimously identify the situation from which Fascism actually originated with the First World War and the crisis that followed it, which was characterized by exceptional economic difficulties, social shifts, the standardization of society, the (bourgeois) resentment for an insufficient victory and the rise of the proletarian movement that was for the most part dominated by the idea of rapidly carrying out in Italy what was achieved in Russia in 1917.

All these elements, which I have merely outlined, as well as others, have provided the basis for the different 'interpretations' of Fascism over the last fifty years. The sense of partiality and insufficiency they have left us with has grown to the point that they have all been refused, explicitly or implicitly, by some historians; according to De Felice, one of the major historians of Fascism, such a refusal was practically translated into:

3 Benedetto Croce, 'Ingenuità dei censori della storia' [The Naivete of the Censors of History], *Quaderni di critica* 6 (November 1946): 102.

> the acceptance of Tasca's assertion that in order to define Fascism, one must above all, write an account of its history. It follows that, in order to write its history, it is necessary to research even the most minute of clues and individual manifestations, including those that might seem irrelevant. This group of scholars has based its research on very extensive and intensive archival investigations.[4]

Looking at it from the outside, it is beyond doubt that this approach has given rise to a profound renewal of the historiography on Fascism, whose complexity and relations it insightfully delineated. But the second part of De Felice's claim remains dubious—that is, the idea according to which in order to write history one needs to proceed with an always more thorough exploration of the archives. Actually, if the exploration of archives is no longer only an indispensable means of research but also its main means or even goal, then it runs the risk of making us lose sight of the objective of 'writing history', which is ultimately to understand how history proceeds in its various moments.

THE FATHERLAND IS DYING

In keeping with this perspective, it is useful to put forward a hypothesis which, moving from well-known and accepted historical elements while arranging them according to a specific *configuration* of forces, can bring us closer to grasping the *real movement* of Fascism's success.

Let us take into consideration the First World War. It is evident that its length, the suffering that accompanied it, the unprecedented massacres it entailed (which cannot at all be compared with the wars of the *Risorgimento*) went far beyond what the nationalist forces—which unleashed it with the 'Radiant Days' of May 1915—could have expected. According to the intention of its proponents, the war should have marked the full achievement of the national ideals

4 De Felice, *Interpretations of Fascism*, pp. 169–70.

pursued for a century; but, eventually, it turned out to be the ruthless demonstration of how these ideals were limited, alien to the masses who had passively been dragged to the slaughterhouse.

The fatherland called for one last war, the definitive one; but war ran the risk of burying forever every ideal of the fatherland for those who personally suffered it. Only this suffering enables us to explain those recurrent episodes in the post-war years when, at the hands of anarchists and communists, the Italian flag was torn and spat on, public officials as well as decorated and even mutilated soldiers were beaten, precisely because they stood for *symbols* of a fatherland that had betrayed its sons, and had now to be considered dead—or murdered.[5]

At the same time, those who directly identified with the ideal of fatherland and participated in it began to entertain the idea—strongly favoured by the rulers[6]—that the 'mutilated' victory caused by former allies and internal 'traitors' could not pay back the great suffering they had undergone, and therefore that the fatherland had been damaged, trampled on, and its life was in danger.

The immediate post-war era in Italy was thus swept by an image of the fatherland as threatened, dead or close to dying—in turn, predictably accompanied by an image of the collapse of the other *values* normally associated with that of the fatherland.

However, we should note that the death of the fatherland was for many veterans, former interventionists and assault infantrymen an event *equally feared and longed for*. Feared insofar as the death of the fatherland meant for them the loss of the supreme value for which they had fought as well as their uprooting from the ground on which they had grown up and in which they recognized themselves. Longed

5 Gaetano Salvemini remarks that 'many veterans, who would have keenly fraternized with the most radical "war socialists", became "anti-Bolshevik" following this stupid brutality, which damaged the revolutionary parties more than any violence and disorder'—*Scritti sul fascismo* [Writings on Fascism], VOL. 1 (Milan: Feltrinelli, 1961), p. 34.

6 Salvemini, *Scritti sul fascismo*, pp. 5–6, p. 446 ff.

for (or even *fulfilled* in fantasies) since it was precisely the fatherland that was the cause and origin of the unprecedented—and mostly useless—suffering they had been subjected to during the war. All in all, I am postulating the presence of a knot of contradictory feelings towards the fatherland precisely in those who were most attached to its value. Remaining within tradition meant remaining faithful to a secure and yet outdated identity, paid with the most difficult personal sacrifices. Parting ways with it certainly meant entering the reality of a world that was alive, open, problematic, but without any guarantee for traditional identity or protection. An inextricable entanglement emerged, which, in the most extreme cases, could certainly make the following paradox evident: those who most loved the fatherland also hated it the most.[7]

THE FASCIST AMALGAM

It seems to me that this hypothesis is directly confirmed by the incredible *amalgam* of socio-political tendencies and approaches that characterized early Fascism, that of 1919–20, before it was supplemented with a brutal 'agrarian' component. We cannot escape the fact that there are clear left-wing elements in it (the call for a constituent assembly; proclamation of the republic; abolition of the Senate, nobility titles, and compulsory military service; disarmament; popular election of the judiciary; suppression of the stock exchange; confiscation of non-productive capital; distribution of land to the peasants; and so on).[8]

7 The presence of this kind of entanglement often lies at the origins of the surprising 'conversions'—characterized as actual 'betrayals' by the supporters of the abandoned cause—that can be observed in leading figures within ideological, religious and political conflicts. There is an extensive phenomenology, open to the most different solutions: suffice it to think of, on the one hand, Saint Paul, who from being a persecutor of Christianity became its Apostle and martyr; on the other, Mussolini himself, who left the field of revolutionary socialism and embraced that of its most resolute opponents (see the next section, and note 10 on p. 84).

8 Salvemini, *Scritti sul fascismo*, pp. 9–10; De Felice, *Mussolini il rivoluzionario* [Mussolini the Revolutionary] (Turin: Einaudi, 1965), p. 513 ff.

After all, this national-revolutionary amalgam pre-existed Fascism in the strict sense; it was already present, in various ways, in left-wing interventionism during the years that immediately preceded the war, which merged with Mussolini's newspaper *Popolo d'Italia* and played a key role, together with Irredentism, in the initial support for war by intellectuals and the petite bourgeoisie.

At that point, Mussolini could write that 'after the great war, the working masses that today merge with the Nation, will request concrete social reforms in the belligerent States—for they will throw away their own lives. These reforms will have to be granted, or else riots will break out'. Three years later, at the onset of the Russian revolution, he could still affirm that the 'unnecessary, even artificial, antithesis between revolution and war' had been solved; 'it is revolution that does not fear war; it is war that saves Revolution'.[9]

For a long time there has been a tendency, especially among the opponents of Fascism, to consider these revolutionary motifs of the Fascist programme as rather insignificant, hardly influential, if not as a pure deceit aimed at misleading the masses that were pushing for socialism.[10]

With hindsight, it instead seems to me that these motifs appear as one of the major causes of both the specific difficulties the political forces of the time experienced in defining and understanding Fascism and of the latter's victory.

9 Quoted in Domenico Settembrini, *Fascismo come controrivoluzione imperfetta* [Fascism as Imperfect Counter-revolution] (Florence: Sansoni, 1978), pp. 46–7. Mussolini makes a similar point in 1919, at the time of the foundation of the *Fasci di Combattimento*: 'We interventionists are the only ones who have the right to speak of revolution in Italy. In May 1915 [. . .] we witnessed the first episode of revolution. That was the beginning. Revolution continued under the name of war for forty months. It has not ended'—quoted in Nicola Tranfaglia, 'E Mussolini chiamò a raccolta' [When Mussolini Called a Rally], *La Repubblica* (18–19 March 1979).

10 This tendency is paralleled by another that interprets Mussolini's behaviour, when he left the editorship of the *Avanti!* for the *Popolo d'Italia*, in terms of sheer 'double-crossing' and 'betrayal' caused by 'bourgeois corruption'. In this vein, see especially Gherardo Bozzetti's book *Mussolini direttore dell'Avanti!'* [Mussolini Editor of *Avanti!*] (Milan: Feltrinelli, 1979), p. 243 ff.

If Fascism had *only* been the 'white guard' of Italian capitalists and agrarians, or simply a reactionary movement based on nationalism, it could not have found the support it actually had, and which pure nationalism never enjoyed. We could even suggest that Fascism had this support *in spite of* its visible and speedy transformation into the *white guard* of those interests.

Ultimately, early Fascism was not only the armed branch of reaction; neither was it only a revolutionary movement in a clear and explicit sense—as some people at times believed,[11] seeing Mussolini as an authentic Italian Lenin, more human and concrete, as somebody put it more recently.[12]

There was in Fascism a real mixture of antithetical thrusts. Both the hypothesis I referred to—that of the feared and longed-for death of the value of fatherland—and the specific 'solution' that originated from it—subsequently called 'Fascism' throughout the twentieth century—are based on this living coexistence of opposites in the early programme of Fascism as well as in its leaders. All in all, it is a matter of understanding how the specific 'bivalence' of Fascism managed to be successful nationwide *precisely as a bivalence*,[13] which was shared by broad masses of young people who were active and sincerely yearned for change.

THE FATHERLAND MUST NOT DIE: THE FATHERLAND BECOMES ROMAN

It seems to me that the decisive moment of this 'solution' was an extremely violent and desperate *denial* of the death of the fatherland. We claimed that such a death was taking place precisely among

11 See for example Salvemini, *Scritti sul fascismo*, pp. 460–1.

12 Settembrini, *Fascismo come controrivoluzione imperfetta*, pp. 15–17 and *passim.*

13 The expression is not derived from Freud or some other psychoanalyst, as one might suppose, but from one of the foremost historians of Fascism, Angelo Tasca. See *Nascita e avvento del fascismo* [Birth and Rise of Fascism], VOL. 1 (Bari: Laterza, 1974), p. 53 ff.

those who were most attached to the fatherland; in order to be effective, its denial involved a radical shift in the ideal of the fatherland towards a field of absoluteness that was previously unknown.

I think it is impossible to compare the intensity of the patriotism Italians learnt to nurture throughout the *Risorgimento* with the cult of the Fatherland established during Fascism. During the *Risorgimento*, the memories of the past, faced with the divisions and subjections of the present, encouraged a struggle that aimed at making the country reach the level of other European nations, which the Italians felt themselves to be potentially equal to and worthy of, although in practice recognizing their inferiority. With Fascism, the ideal of the fatherland became an exclusive and intolerant totality, thanks to the ever-increasing assumption of a monumental *Romanitas*.

It is not a coincidence that Fascism took *Romanitas* as a fundamental point of reference. Any other prevailing reference to different Italian historical periods—for instance, the *Risorgimento* that immediately preceded it and Garibaldi's Expedition of the Thousand, or the Renaissance of Machiavelli and the *Condottieri*—would have been insufficient, too localized and narrow-minded, for the attempted Resurrection of the fatherland. Something gigantic and boundless was needed, a sort of undefined and mythical vault that could cover the horizon as a whole without leaving any gap. Such a compactness of the mythical heavens, ensured by *Romanitas*, was far more important than the fact that very few Italians were initially able to identify themselves with the distant deeds of the Romans.

In the name and on behalf of this total and exclusive fatherland—which was indeed gradually built, or better, divined and revealed—Fascists could proceed, with equanimity and without hesitation, to the extermination of those 'without a country'—that is, all the people who were concretely alien to nationalist ideology, such as Communists and Socialists. In the name of the supreme Law of the fatherland, by punishing their opponents, the Fascists even managed to suppress their own fantasies about killing the fatherland.

THE RITUALS OF THE FATHERLAND

While the first part of their operation was successful in an almost perfect way—within a few years, there was no real obstacle opposing the establishment of the dictatorship—the same did not hold for the second. In fact, one does not need to look too far to see that the total fatherland Fascists had erected turned out to be a cardboard facade, the shell of a void, of an irremediable absence.

Whence the necessity of continuous and omnipresent *rituals* that reaffirmed the existence and greatness of the fatherland, against the continuous re-emergence of doubts about its degradation. When they were successful, these rituals undoubtedly established, for a few hours, a solid and passionate intimacy between the masses, the people and the fatherland as visibly embodied by the *Duce*. They temporarily reconstituted a total and mythical unity within a *time of return*—as happened when (and this was perhaps the supreme moment) the great enchanter evoked the presence on the 'fateful hills' of a resurrected and physically present Roman Empire . . .[14] But, in the long run, this was essentially a desperate task: the rituals themselves were undone by boredom and emptiness; they had to become compulsory through 'draft-cards' . . .

Something more—something stronger and *definitive*—was always needed. At bottom, from this perspective, the Fascist wars were themselves ritual wars, extreme rituals; they were devoid of urgent economic and political significance and instead loaded with a mythical duty of restoration. The (public, nocturnal) declaration of war—'in the skies of Rome'—was already as such a great ceremonial event, as much as the declaration of the end of war. One could say that it was more important than the conflict itself, which as such—to the extent that it involved great masses of people—was exorcized and propitiated through the invocation of the 'proletarian nation'.

14 [A reference to a speech delivered by Mussolini on 9 May 1936 from the balcony of Palazzo Venezia celebrating the recent victory in Ethiopia, in which he declared 'the reappearance of the Empire on the fatal hills of Rome'—Trans.]

It was the 'proletarian nation' that had to defend, and possibly expand, the 'sacred soil' of the fatherland, the 'untouchable borders' of the Empire. The 'second soul' of Fascism resurfaced here. And, obviously, this is where the disaster took place.

When the crusade against those 'without a country'—identified, at the same time, with the 'Bolsheviks' and the 'plutocratic democracies'—clashed against real and insurmountable difficulties—that is, when Italy entered the Second World War—the cardboard facade suddenly collapsed and revealed the empty void behind it. In this sense, it is true that Fascism was a 'parenthesis' in the history of Italy: for twenty years, it prevented people from seeing and recognizing the death of the nineteenth-century values on which Italian unification had been built, a death that was actually already evident at the end of the First World War. When Fascism fell, Italy faced the problems that had already tragically surfaced twenty years earlier—in the first place, that of the huge masses alien to the ethical and political orientations of a small ruling class.

Defeat in the Second World War was a liberating event, because it enabled the emergence of these forces, whereas, on the contrary, *victory* in the First World War plunged Italy into two decades during which a mythical past ruled over people.[15]

15 Some of the common elements we have recovered in this Fascist *configuration* can also be found in the origins and development of Nazism. A tendency that amalgamated 'revolutionary' and nationalist orientations developed in a country that had undergone the catastrophic collapse of a longstanding attempt at hegemonizing Europe and was suffering a profound economic crisis. There was a racist and anti-Semitic component in this nationalist orientation that was unknown to Italian nationalism. The Germany taken as a central point of reference was not Bismarck's Germany (notwithstanding its glories) nor Frederick the Great's Prussia. It was instead a mythical State devoted to the triumph of the Aryan Northern-Germanic race over all other races, a race from which the culture and civilization of our continent was mythically supposed to derive. This orientation was rapidly successful and strengthened through the organization of extraordinary rallies, clearly inspired by theatre and religion, which magically made present the greatness of Germany to all participants. It is significant that, for Hitler, the

preparation of these rallies, their style and symbolism, and the kind of oratory to be used were a major preoccupation since the beginning of his political activity (see Chapter 12 of his *Mein Kampf*). After the seizure of power, these rallies took on the appearance of an actual liturgy, whose central and 'definitive' rituals were the ceremonies on Heroes' Memorial Day and the March of German Youth in Nuremberg (see George Lachmann Mosse, *The Nationalization of the Masses: Political Symbolism and Mass Movements in Germany from the Napoleonic Wars through the Third Reich* [New York; Howard Fertig, 1975], p. 83). We could go as far as attributing to these two central events the meaning of a ritual dedicated to the living-dead on the one hand, and to the initiation of the young on the other. The project of a full mythical restoration of the German Fatherland, devastated after the First World War, is always prominently present in the annexations, conquests and wars of Nazism. By unveiling these common elements, I do not intend to enter the dispute, by now classical among historians, about the affinities and differences between Fascism and Nazism. There are actual differences, and they are huge. But the fact remains that in both cases we witness the triggering of a *configuration* of forces that is extremely distinctive.

VII
SUGGESTIONS AND CONCLUSIONS

SPECIFIC AND REPEATABLE

Historians have long been aware of the violent contrasts that, in post-World War I Italy, assembled around the value of the fatherland and of the gradual affirmation, through Fascism, of a hyper-patriotic ideology that, at the same time, intended to answer the emerging demands of the masses of people who had been excluded or sacrificed in the name of this very same value. They have also considered the rituals and events officiated by the *Duce* and his lieutenants.

I have here gathered these elements in a way that composes them as a set, that is, a significant configuration capable of grasping what I think is an essential aspect of the Fascist situation. A problem regarding death connected to an element that has a highly symbolic meaning—the fatherland—is confronted in a peculiar way due to the highly contradictory relation entertained with it by those obliged to confront it. A movement denying the death of the fatherland and the transference of this symbol into a field of abstract absoluteness originates from an unsolvable dilemma, as an immediate solution that is nevertheless endowed with incalculable consequences. What surfaces here in a noticeable way is a time of (cyclical) return; actual rituals of a patriotic cult emerge and involve all aspects of life (from the daily greeting in the name of the *Duce* to the 'oceanic rallies' and Fascist wars). They are not ornamental or gratuitous but amount to an intimate necessity of Fascism which essentially coexists with the very reasons that made it successful as a collective force.

At this point we must clearly acknowledge that the configuration of forces we have outlined is specifically Fascist; it is part of a precise and delimited historical framework. It seems that we cannot be accused of forcing things historically. And yet, as noted, we have unveiled a similar configuration, in completely different circumstances, in other situations, such as those of the obsessional and the archaic. This does not at all imply that these situations are identical. We cannot and must not confuse obsessional neurotics, archaic people and Fascists. But the fact remains that there is a germinal configuration they all share.

CATASTROPHES OF THE SACRED

Within the specificity of each configuration there also remains a common movement. A value-figure is saved through its transposition onto a different field; this involves its actual transformation, the passage into another form *irreducible to the one that precedes it. Thus a genuine qualitative leap takes place, or, if we wish to use a different—and less philosophically charged—terminology, a genuine 'catastrophe'.*[1]

We must now name this transformed situation and circumscribe the set of transpositions and subsequent transformations it triggers.

Undoubtedly, such a term already exists, namely, the sacred—*which already surfaced in the course of the present work. What we witness in each of the configurations we analysed is, precisely, a* catastrophe of the sacred.

I am certain that introducing the word 'sacred' in my research will surprise some readers. As is well known, it is a word that is constantly used in confused and tendentious ways. I therefore wish to specify that I intend to use it only with reference to a set *of characteristics or qualities that we have observed, in varying degrees and numbers, in the situations we have analysed, and which are also found*

1 I use the term 'catastrophe' in the sense of a sharp transformation, or sudden discontinuity, as it is used in René Thom's mathematical theory. The latter is indeed called 'catastrophe theory'. See René Thom, *Structural Stability and Morphogenesis* (Boulder CO: Westview Press, 1994); *Mathematical Models of Morphogenesis* (Hemel Hempstead: Ellis Horwood, 1984). See also Erik Christopher Zeeman, *Catastrophe Theory: Selected Papers* (Reading MA: Addison-Wesley, 1977). For the time being, I leave open the question as to whether applying Thom's theory to this field could be useful.

in the phenomenology of the sacred as usually understood: from majestic and ultra-powerful authority to the terrifying-persecutory, from the horrible to the fascinating, and so on. In other words, I rely on a set of common elements, one that circumscribes the phenomenology of the sacred and turns it into an inevitable term, if we want to avoid squandering a series of very distinctive experiences by consigning them to the generic categories of the ideological and the symbolic.

Now, the difficulty of every cognitive effort in this field of interest does not originate, in the first place, from the well-known multiplicity and variability of sacred phenomena.[2] *Instead, it originates especially from the fact that most of the characterizations that have been attempted so far connect from the outset* the sacred with religion—*whether in a negative or positive sense, in a strict manner or in terms of a simple 'aura'.*

For example, let us consider what is perhaps the most renowned work in this field, namely, Rudolf Otto's Das Heilige (The Idea of the Holy), *which has been published in dozens of editions and regularly appears in every article or book devoted to this topic. At first sight, one is struck by the freedom with which this investigation moves, in spite of belonging to the field of theology in the strict sense. In his characterizations of the sacred, Otto does not shy away from dwelling on those of its aspects that appear to be most provocative for common religious consciousness: namely, the repulsive, terrifying and horrific aspects that produce in those who experience them a relationship dominated by atonement and propitiation. He does not even shy away from clearly indicating the contradictory aspects contained by the sacred, for instance, its being both repellent and fascinating.*[3]

However, such a freedom of movement appears to be neutralized by a preliminary assumption, namely, the fact that one would come upon the sacred only

2 Mircea Eliade, *Patterns in Comparative Religions* (New York: Sheed & Ward, 1958): 'We cannot be sure that there is *anything*—object, movement, psychological function, being or even game—that has not at some time in human history been somewhere transformed into a hierophany. It is a very different matter to find out *why* that particular thing should have become a hierophany, or should have stopped being one at any given moment. But it is quite certain that anything man has ever handled, felt, come in contact with or loved *can* become a hierophany' (p. 11).

3 Rudolf Otto, *The Idea of the Holy: An Inquiry into the Non-Rational Factor in the Idea of the Divine and Its Relation to the Rational* (Oxford: Oxford University Press, 1936), pp. 31–41.

in the religious field, for it amounts to the intimate essence of every religion. From this assumption follows a subtle and at times almost imperceptible religious translation of the whole phenomenology of the sacred. The sensation of mysterium tremendum, *of something hidden or a terrifying secret, which belongs to the experience of the sacred, thus becomes 'that which is mysterious* [. . .] *in a* religious *sense* [. . .] *the wholly other'.*[4] *The feeling of dependence, which, according to Schleiermacher, is fundamental in the experience of the sacred, and which as such highlights the fundamental position of those who experience it, is replaced by the feeling of being a creature, 'the feeling of creaturehood, that is, the consciousness of the littleness of every creature* in face of that which is above all creatures'*; as such, this feeling would be the* consequence *of the feeling that there exists a subject outside the self.*[5]

It is the presupposed existence of the divine as an independent entity, or religion's ontological leap, *that implicitly ends up regulating the observation of the sacred. In this way, it is easy to operate a schematization or forcing of the situations that are being described. The most dreadful aspects of the sacred, and the very feeling of 'dread'—which is acknowledged by Otto as fundamental to this experience—are included in a developmental scale, one in which they turn out to be 'overborne and ousted by more highly developed forms of the numinous emotion'.*[6] *A widespread and problematic phenomenology of the sacred—which even manages to permeate the most immediate and intense ways of conceiving the divine (Yahweh as angered, jealous, and as a god of danger and persecution . . .)—is thus underestimated and reduced to a raw and primitive moment of experience.*

4 Otto, *The Idea of the Holy*, p. 26.

5 Otto, *The Idea of the Holy*, p. 22 [emphasis added]. In this light, the example with which Otto introduces the 'feeling of creatorhood' is quite curious. He refers to the words with which Abraham addresses God (*Genesis*, 18, 27)—'Behold now, I have taken upon me to speak onto the Lord, which am but dust and ashes'—when he ventures to plead with Him for the people of Sodom and Gomorra after God communicated him his intention to destroy the two cities. In this context, 'dust' and 'ashes' correspond to Abraham's identification with the inhabitants of the cities that God threatens to burn down. He is not hopeful when he addresses the creator; instead, he asks the destroyer to be compassionate. The sense of impotence and dependence that Otto criticizes prevails in Abraham's stance.

6 Otto, *The Idea of the Holy*, p. 16.

In short, the sacred—which Otto acknowledges in its divergent expressions (from the numinous to the repellent, the majestic and energetic to the terrifying)—is entirely channelled and, we could add, abducted by the field of established religion. This kind of operation is often carried out also by those who, moving from presuppositions that are external or contrary to religion, end up assessing the sacred in a way that is far more reductive that the theistic one proposed by Otto.

Now, the fundamental fact we should stress is that the sacred does not *coincide with religion as a separate institution, an institution specializing in divine matters. In the life of archaic people, the sacred greatly exceeds the domain* we *are used to assign to religious experience and theory.*[7] *On the other hand, there are religions in which the sacred does not play an essential role—for instance, Confucianism.*[8] *But the most persuasive proof for this distinction is provided by a comparative linguistic examination of the terms used for the notions of sacred, divine and religion.*

In the Indo-European context,[9] *the examination of the terms with which we designate the sacred indicates at the same time their 'antiquity and etymological disparity'. In many languages, there are complementary terms* (hierós *and* hágios *in Greek;* sacer *and* sanctus *in Latin, etc.) from which it is nonetheless impossible to derive a unitary model. For instance, the well-known twofold value of* sacer*—which means both 'profane' and 'contaminated', 'venerable' and 'cursed'—is not present in the Greek* hierós. *Ultimately, there is thus no 'common prehistory of the sacred'. At the same time, no term related to god is bound to* sacer *or* hierós*: 'We are dealing with two different notions.' The notion of god refers back to 'luminous' or 'celestial', as opposed to man as 'terrestrial' (this is what the Latin* homo *means). As for the notion of religion, in the Indo-European context, there exists no common term for it, and, even after the advent of writing, several languages do not have it; this should not surprise us if we take into account the fact that 'one can clearly conceive and hence name religion only starting from*

7 Eliade, *Patterns in Comparative Religions*, p. 30 ff.

8 Marcel Granet, *The Religion of the Chinese People* (Oxford: Basil Blackwell, 1975), Chapter 3.

9 Émile Benveniste, *Dictionary of Indo-European Concepts and Society* (Chicago: University of Chicago Press, 2016); see chapters 'The "Sacred"' and 'Religion and Superstition'.

the moment in which it is delimited, has a distinctive field, and one can know what belongs to it and what does not'.

In the case of Hebrew, the etymology of qadôš *is uncertain; some scholars link it to the root* qd(d), *that is, 'separated'; others to* quddušu, *that is, 'brilliant', 'pure'. However, in both cases one observes an evolution of the concept, which 'moves from purely magical values, related to Power, to ethical and historical ones'. That is, the Prophets set aside the concept and apply it to the presence of God in the history of Israel, 'in the complex sense according to which Gods sanctifies himself by electing Israel and turns Israel, his people, into the holy people'. 'However, in linguistic use the original and magical implications of the term are still present in noticeable forms.'*[10]

As for the Polynesian term mana*—which can be listed under the general category of Power and therefore ascribed to the sacred, along with its 'equivalents'* wakan, orenda, manitu *present among other populations—we know only too well how much it was abused by an academic debate that started at the end of the nineteenth century and lasted for decades. Linguistic observations are much more precious than the 'animistic' or 'pre-animistic' hypotheses that have plagued Western culture.* Mana *'is a noun, an adjective and a verb'*[11] *and operates as an 'algebraic symbol' in order to 'represent an indeterminate value of signification';*[12] *the Sioux's* wakan *is used in a 'protean' way as both a noun and an adjective and as such implies an indeterminate representation; the* mulungu *of the Bantu languages originally refers to the place of the ancestors' spirits and subsequently to the power that is exercized there.*[13]

From all this we can deduce that the sacred—characterized by an extraordinary phenomenal multiplicity—is different from religion—understood as a separate institution and a complex organization of widespread hypostasized

10 See Alfonso Maria Di Nola, 'Sacro e profano' in *Enciclopedia delle religioni*, VOL. 5 (Florence: Vallecchi, 1973), p. 680 ff.

11 Marcel Mauss, *A General Theory of Magic* (London and New York: Routledge, 2001), p. 133.

12 Claude Lévi-Strauss, *Introduction to the Work of Marcel Mauss* (London: Routledge & Kegan Paul, 1987), p. 55.

13 Ernst Cassirer, *Language and Myth* (New York: Dover Publications, 1946), pp. 69–71.

positions.[14] *The sacred precedes religion and is subsequently channelled by it to the point where the two become almost equivalent in collective consciousness. It is the latter that enabled scholars such as Otto to start off their investigation from an assumption that actually cannot withstand historical-linguistic scrutiny.*

If we accept this approach, that is, separate the sacred from its religious vicissitudes in a strict sense in order to restore its ubiquity, it is easy to see how the manner in which I have used the term in the present work is not arbitrary. It perfectly corresponds to the various stages of the archaic transformation of the dead into ancestors, and the related issues we delineated. But it is equally easy to see that it can also be adapted to the case of obsession; in its strictly speaking phobic and obsessive creations, we find again that coexistence of horror and fascination, those aspects of terror and annulment before a majestic authority, and a correlative attitude of propitiation-expiation, as pointed out by Otto. We are dealing with aspects that are also present, in varying degrees, in the archaic transformation, but for the obsessional they constitute the framework of a, so to speak, private *sacred—paraphrasing Freud's well-known formula according to which obsessional neurosis is a 'private religion'—whose contents are certainly not comprehensible and transmissible to others but which is rigorously a form of sacredness from the standpoint of the one who lives it.*

This stance allows us to rapidly clarify some questions that have remained open. If obsession is rightly posited on its own ground as an experience of the sacred, then Freud's comparing it with religion is to say the least partial. In his work dedicated to this theme,[15] *Freud particularly insists on the similarities between obsessive ceremonials and behaviours on the one hand, and religious practices on the other. What is in this way brought together is a* ritualistic religion *which, although it has different deities and cults, belongs to both obsessionals and*

14 Here I am not referring only to the stage of 'temporary deities' but, more generally, to that level of experience where 'the creative act, while it is in progress, is not recognized as such [. . .] All spontaneity is felt as receptivity, all creativity as being, and every product of subjectivity as so much substantiality'—Cassirer, *Language and Myth*, pp. 61–2). Cassirer specifically examines the hypostasis of technical action and speech.

15 Sigmund Freud, 'Obsessive Actions and Religious Practices', SE, VOL. 9, pp. 115–28 / *GW*, VOL. 7, pp. 129–39.

non-obsessionals: from the pious to the scrupulous, all the way up to Confucians. But we could say that this does not do justice either to obsessionals or non-obsessional religious people insofar as the dimension of the sacred, present in these two situations, is indeed overlooked.

This nonchalance is quite recurrent in Freud's work. While his interest in religion is explicit and even increasing—from The Future of an Illusion *to the late* Moses and Monotheism*—we could suggest that his interest in the sacred is rigorously taboo . . . Indeed, facing the concept of taboo, Freud seems to be moving as if he were confronting something remote and difficult to comprehend and visible only in obsessionals. Thus the extensive treatment devoted to the* Unheimliche *as what is perturbing or uncanny—one of the essential aspects of the numinous experience—mostly takes place within, in a broad sense, aesthetic or narrative considerations.*[16]

This obliteration of the sacred does not originate from Freud's self-avowed 'special obtuseness' with regard to the uncanny,[17] *or from a concern, typical of the Enlightenment, to avoid the field of the enemy—religion—which has historically monopolized the sacred. Instead, it originates from the impossibility of conceiving, in his theoretical terms, the qualitative leap or catastrophe that the concept of the sacred requires. I stress again that the sacred is posited by Freud as a problem that emerges from the themes of his clinical work with obsessionals, not from his separate considerations on religion.*

In his own theoretical terms, Freud was obliged to emphasize the absolute continuity between the personal, and concretely individual, problems of obsessionals-to-be and their obsessive transposition. In this way, he walked into a trap symmetrical to the one von Gebsattel fell prey to: the former stressed a reductive and misleading continuity; the latter highlighted an abstract separation. Freud erased the sacred, whereas von Gebsattel would have extolled it, if he had not been hindered by a traditional and high-flown conception of it.

We still have to consider the third case, namely, Fascism. While in obsessionals the sacred pervades the unfolding of a childhood event—essentially, an individual development arrested at its outset—in Fascism, we witness an attempt,

16 Sigmund Freud, 'The "Uncanny"' in *SE*, VOL. 17 (1917–1919), pp. 217–56 / *GW*, VOL. 12, pp. 227–68.

17 Freud, 'The "Uncanny"', *SE*, VOL. 17, p. 220 / *GW*, VOL. 12, pp. 230–1.

perhaps the clearest in modern times, to sacralize *the history of numerous human beings, depriving it of an independent, immanent, and only partially foreseeable logic, and including their lives into another time.*

In the previous section, I outlined the fundamental elements of Fascist ritualism. The sacred as the fascinating horror induced by an uncontrollable power was present and active in Fascism—perhaps only at its beginnings—through the dark evocation of death which was at the same time despised. The black colour of uniforms and flags as well as the use of funereal symbols such as skulls and crossbones intended violently to affirm the death threat of a power that dominated and defeated death itself.[18]

At a later stage, the aspect of absolute power prevailed in Fascism. In this regard, we should highlight an element that turns out to be totally consistent with the phenomenology of the sacred and, at the same time, appeared to be an original invention of Fascism. I am referring to the Duce's words, *his speeches broadcast by the radio, and listened to by the entire nation. While a plethora of professors were busy analysing and praising their 'chiselled' style, which was compared to that of Julius Caesar, the most 'incisive' sentences were engraved or painted on the walls of houses, in both cities and the countryside, so that they could constantly stand as a warning, stimulus and threat for everyone.*

Now, 'Believe, Obey, Fight!' and all the mottos that were coercively imposed on every sighted person, just as the radio speeches were imposed on every hearing person, certainly represented an early example of political power's unscrupulous and totalitarian use of the modern technologies of propaganda. This is an aspect that has been widely pointed out.[19] *Yet we should also add that, in the* Duce's

18 Along these lines, Fascism was far outstripped by its younger sibling and major pupil, German Nazism. It seems to me beyond doubt that, in Germany, facing a political order that promised the 'Thousand-Year Reich', a whole nation managed to live that mixture of terror and fascination typical of some forms of the sacred. Possibly, the subsequent mass-repression was proportional in its intensity to that of participation. (In Italy, repression gave way to a persistent anti-Fascist ideology that carried out a similar function of estrangement and protection.)

19 In this regard, see Philip V. Cannistraro's excellent, *La fabbrica del consenso. Fascismo e mass media* [The Factory of Consent: Fascism and Mass Media] (Bari: Laterza, 1975). On the construction of the myth of Mussolini, see pp. 80–4. It is likely that Mussolini understood the importance of the radio even before knowing what to do

speeches, his word tended to recover that position of self-sufficiency, power and inherent effectiveness that is typical of the sacred word. From this perspective, the radio did not give rise to a flow *of scattered words; on the contrary, it broadcast a* full speech, *that is, a solid* word that lasts, *fittingly aimed at being engraved on the walls of houses and the pediments of monuments. The radio stood for the magical procedure that gave access to majestic language and made it possible to sense it in its omnipotent unfolding. The modern cult of Mussolini's word was therefore, at the same time, an archaic ritual; it was the evocation of the word and name of a god which, as we saw, are often more active and powerful among archaic people than the god himself. Perhaps more than elsewhere, it is here that Fascism's intense aspiration to numinous force and energy was realized.*

Returning to the other situation we analysed, this force and energy are present in obsessionals only in a negative way, as an omnipotent yet terrifying and destructive word, which one is thus compelled to monitor rigorously. Using a couple of categories identified by ethnological research, we could suggest that while obsessionals are confined to the taboo *word, that is, the negative aspect of the force of the sacred, the Fascist word at times managed to reach the dimension of* mana *and its affirmative force.*[20]

It is true that these attempts to achieve a sacred power turned out to be vain and transient. As we have noted, the historical moment that enabled their emergence was exceptional and could not last long or immediately be repeated—precisely because it was part of a different logic. But it would be wrong to consider Fascist 'mourning' as a mere theatrical stroke of genius by Mussolini and his followers, and the use of radio speeches as an intelligent employment of mass media. It is clear that this 'mourning' and those speeches soon became the cornerstone of a sham, a repetitive mass spectacle. But this impasse of the sacred elements and of the sacred itself—often reduced to its most threatening and openly persecutory components—does not go against the sacred as such.

with it. As early as 1923, he rejected a proposal for a private national network sponsored by Guglielmo Marconi himself and, thanks to a legislative decree, reserved for the state any future system of wireless communication (p. 226).

20 In this light, Hitler's speeches could possibly reveal interesting elements of similarity and difference with Mussolini's. Perhaps the majestic, terrifying, and persecutory aspect turns out to be more pronounced in the former.

Indeed, the sacred is always on the verge of an impasse. In this work, I have repeatedly pointed to the precariousness of the solutions achieved. Like a tightrope walker, archaic society is always in a precarious situation with regard to its own norms and the government of the living-dead. Its rituals can in the long run appear to be desperate. The obsessional himself partly embodies this desperate ritualization. Fascist despair, already present in its initial 'mourning', was made explicit during war and destruction. But a threatening crisis is latent in every sacred 'thing' or 'situation', like a thin crack threatens thick ice. And it could not be otherwise, considering that the experience of the sacred does not lie, as often believed, in the 'thing' or 'situation', that is, in the instance of presence and the very presence of the 'radically other'. Rather, it is to be found in the totally singular approach of those who live it, in an always renewed and changing flux that comes back to people without them recognizing it as such. It is therefore necessary to admit that the sacred, precisely as a well-defined experience, is not combined with the eternal but with the ephemeral; it takes flight, instead of dwelling in the places where one encountered it and where several people would like to secure it forever. Against the tendency of those who endeavour to grant the sacred a kind of full and solid existence opposed to the fragility of the modern world, it is necessary to recall that the sacred is not only fragile but, at each turn, *partial, refracted, and displaced. There is no eclipse of the sacred; the sacred itself is continuously at the margins of its own eclipse.*[21]

21 I am referring to Sabino Samuele Acquaviva's well-known book, *L'eclissi del sacro nella civiltà occidentale* [The Eclipse of the Sacred in Western Civilization] (Milan: Comunità, 1966). Like Otto, Acquaviva identifies the sacred with religion, and the latter's historical decadence is therefore read as an eclipse or a potentially unstoppable crisis of the sacred as such. According to Jean Baudrillard, the act of 'symbolic exchange'—which embraces both the sacred and magic—seems to have the texture of a primitive, if not primordial, 'undivided word' (*Symbolic Exchange and Death*, p. 222) which is at the same time an 'absolute law' valid at all times and in every society (p. 134). The impasses of this word or absolute law are thus in general completely overlooked (see, for instance, with regard to the frequent impasse in the relationship with the dead, the hasty footnote on p. 189). However, we should specify that, for Baudrillard, there also seems to be another conception of the symbolic. Following an original reading of Saussure's *Cahiers d'Anagrammes*, the symbolic act of poetry would consist of an annulment and full exhaustion of the linguistic signifier by means of rigorous procedures, such as

THE ONE AND THE MANY

We have explained a series of processes that, under certain conditions, are common to both individuals and society. It may seem that in doing so we are eliminating every basic difference between the two, whereby data that can be observed in one field would easily be applicable to the other.

It is certainly the case that, quoting a historian, 'society and the individual are inseparable; they are necessary and complementary to each other, not opposites'.[22] We can all agree with that, but we also need to clarify in which way and through what specifications such a complementarity takes place. Otherwise, we run the risk of making the usual mistake of mechanically and automatically transferring data derived from the individual to society and vice versa. This is what one normally observes in many books of psychoanalysis and sociology, in which the casual passage I have just referred to ends up giving rise to a recurrent and dull discontent and finally a sense of unsolved theoretical difficulty.

We should stress that this difficulty is not solved even by those who accept and posit a difference in principle between individual and society, and therefore turn with equanimity to one or the other by considering them as self-sufficient elements that are logically indifferent to one another. This separation—especially frequent in academic research—seems mostly based on the implicit construction of a (prescientific and ultimately metaphysical) *barrier* such as the following: on the one hand, there is the autonomous and sovereign individual; on the other, society, which is equally autonomous and

those enacted in the primitive gift-exchange. In this sense, the poetic is the place of our ambivalence (and not simply ambiguity) with regard to language (p. 219). Obviously, the outcome of this operation is uncertain. We should also notice that this poetic symbol is never a new totalization, or a resurrection of a given identity, but a one-way dispersal, dissemination and diffraction through poetry (pp. 205–07). In this case, it therefore seems that Baudrillard is insisting on the *attempt* to construct a non-totalizing symbolic, instead of on the legislative practice of an 'inevitable' symbolic (p. 134 ff.).

22 Edward Hallett Carr, *What Is History?* (Harmondsworth: Penguin, 1987), p. 31.

sovereign. But thanks to the investigations initiated by Freud, the individual atom turns out to be open, ramified towards the outside, that is, society; at the same time, society shows it is less and less supported by those inherent and always valid rules to which positivistic claims wanted to assign the stability of Newtonian laws. *Hypotheses non fingo!*: alas, even here things have changed behind the scene, and the waters are murky. Today the individual turns out to be less accidental than we assumed and society more unplanned and improbable than we could suppose, not only one hundred or fifty years ago but also a decade ago.

We still need to add a couple of words about those who solve the problem by simply denying that it exists, that is, immediately subsuming one of the terms under the other. It seems to me that, in this field, those who privilege the collective term—society—have so far been much more numerous. They have developed actual *sociolatries*, differently specified with regard to their privileged object (the economy, the State, exchange, and so on), but all sharing the disappearance or assimilation into it of the individual term. Such an assimilation should be complete and perfect, given that the individual is posited as inexistent from the outset. And yet, to varying degrees, every *sociolatry* is compelled to acknowledge—if only by means of its macroscopic impasses and blunders—the persistence of a remainder, waste, or at least an illusion that proves to be particularly stubborn and resistant. Some sociolatries are thus indeed tempted to theorize *and practice* the individual as a remainder or waste of the collective process. This does not seem to be a brilliant solution.

SOCIETY AS A *BONHOMME*

Attempting to clarify these problems, I would like to focus on an instance of experience that seems to me to be quite common and capable of challenging a widespread intellectual cliché. If we consider a set of people combined as a group or society—of any epoch and nationality—after a more or less protracted period of time they will appear to us as our fellows, become comprehensible and almost transparent in their behaviours, however enigmatic and strange the latter may initially appear to be. Actually, after an initial stage needed for a necessary adjustment, every tribe or nation will give us the impression that it is not only known but, in a sense, even clear and predictable. In spite of an at-first-sight immense distance in all fields of associated life, every society will end up appearing to us as a sort of *bonhomme* endowed with characteristics that are easily graspable and perceivable. Our thinking about this group or society will soon lose that sense of estrangement that struck us at the beginning and we will feel that immediate familiarity—pleasant but obviously often also unpleasant—with which we live in our own society.

THE END OF MARCO POLO

At this point anyone who has opened an ethnography book will be ready to contest my argument, quoting extremely strange customs, unusual and unexplainable rituals, that is, everything that for our imagination as readers of ethnography books and habitual documentary viewers works as a lure to fantasize about what is different from and alien to us. Inevitably, this kind of reaction is perhaps also present at a first stage of ethnographic research, that of those who, coming back home, gladly assume the envied role of the narrator, or that of Marco Polo who, in front of the astonished Venetians, takes out of the pockets of his worn-out dress all kinds of gems and precious stones. But once this stage is overcome, after the moment of wonder and amazement is over, when the lights of an unachievable distance are turned off, the honest explorer can only speak about himself and ourselves. This lucid and slightly sad awareness clearly emerges from the major texts of ethnography and far surpasses the stunned descriptions of neophytes and journalists, as well as the erudite investigations of Westerners hunting for academic titles. This kind of awareness makes the greatness of Lévi-Strauss' *Tristes Tropiques* and of some diaries written separately from and, one would say, against subsequent public accounts.[23] After all, in order

23 See for instance Malinowski, *A Diary in the Strict Sense of the Term* (New York: Harcourt, Brace & World Inc., 1967).

to grasp this one does not need to spend a whole life in the bush: some Westerners, who were undoubtedly quite sedentary, realized it without leaving their room.[24]

THE 'MADMAN' IS ALWAYS POSSIBLE

While society as a whole thus appears to be more easily graspable in this common experience than it is in scholarly research, the opposite goes for the individual considered as independent. It is certain that for many of us the individual turns out to be more problematic, less easily localizable and circumscribable than specialized research assumes—that is, in the first place, psychological research. Especially after the planetary expansion of psychoanalysis, but also the widespread sociopolitical interpretation of psychiatric disorders, the idea of a perfect knowability of the individual and his 'motivations' has gained consensus, almost as if there were a promise that, in this field, it is or will be possible to reach a full solution for every difficulty. What intervenes here is the impression of an in-depth research that, layer after layer, having descended as far as the foundation of all foundations, resurfaces again with an ultimate and definitive key—as well as the idea of a meticulous geometrical derivation of the individual from his sociohistorical context, which, if applied 'correctly', dissolves his issues without leaving any considerable remainder.

Instead, many people feel that the individual preserves something irreducible, unforeseeable and unsettling. In the tenacious and persistent idea of the 'madman', which continuously circulates in the 'lower' strata of society and resists the anathemas of progressive psychiatrists or anti-psychiatrists, there is not only a bias that is rightly anathematized but also a sedimentation of the profound conviction that the individual—any individual—could *always* 'flip out' [*dar fuori di matto*], suddenly revealing himself to be unpredictable and elusive. And this is the case in spite of the definitely incomprehensible aspects

24 I am referring in particular to Ludwig Wittgenstein, *Remarks on Frazer's Golden Bough* (Retford: Brynmill, 1983): 'We can only *describe* and say, human life is like that' (p. 3).

of madness (such as hallucinations, deliria, obsessions, etc.), which most of us happily delegate to specialists.

THE TYPE OF DIFFERENCE

We therefore find ourselves in a situation antithetical to the one that scholarly consensus takes almost for granted. According to a sort of basic knowledge embedded in common experience, society is an 'easier' topic than the individuals who form it, and, all things considered, something more foreseeable even in its most deplorable and feared developments. Indeed, the latter are usually attributed to the deliria or imprudence of individuals—who were often previously considered as very 'promising'—rather than to anonymous collective processes. This is one of the reasons why, most of the time, the majority of people do not worry about the society in which they live, because it amounts to a familiar background that is quite constant, taking it into consideration only when they are directly interpellated or something gets under their skin.

Instead, in the eyes of scholars interested in society, the topic they handle runs the risk of always seeming more complex and ungraspable. On the other hand, those who study the individual frequently display an attitude of arrogant mastery over their 'matter'. Moreover, due to the relentless multiplication of cultural specializations, the actual division between these two groups of scholars is always more radical, and the individual seems at times to be extremely distant from the society or societies one discusses in books and conferences—and vice versa.

On the contrary, according to that curious basic knowledge I have just evoked, the difference between individual and society always remains a difference of degree, not of principle; in the passage from one term to the other, one does not so much perceive a radical change as a modification, a different application of common forces which are arranged in a different manner in the field of action.

ACTORS AND MISE-EN-SCÈNE

What is then the meaning of this difference? Let us return to the conclusions we drew from our examination of the obsessive situation with respect to archaic people: we said that the obsessional is an archaic micro-society, that is, he embraces a set of different positions that, in the case of archaic people, are instead distributed across different individuals or groups. From this coexistence of more positions within the same person there follows that particular entanglement, laboriousness and incomprehensibility that strikes us in the obsessional and, at first sight, makes any comparison with the archaic people look quite bizarre—even if we are compelled to acknowledge numerous 'agreements' between them. The obsessional is obsessive because he is forced to face alone, within himself, a kind of problem that archaic society can try to solve through an actual distribution of roles. The latter manages to stage on a public scene, dramatize and ritualize before everybody a problem that the obsessional cannot perform, because he is simultaneously every role.

THE UNFOLDING OF POSITIONS

I suggest that we generalize the outcome of this comparison. The difference between individual and society, which is *not eliminable*, is not due to a substantial difference between them. In society, there are no thrusts or tendencies that are different from those we find actualized in the individual. There are no 'social' forces different from 'individual' ones and therefore it is not a question of deriving one from the other, of socializing the individual or psychologizing society. For example, 'desire' is no more an individual fact than 'economy' is a social one. Instead, in society, we find an *unfolded* series of positions that the individual necessarily concentrates within himself; this unfolding into the various articulations of society enables us to understand quite effortlessly a set of problems that, because of the forced interpenetrations of these very positions, turn out to be ungraspable in the individual.

This is the reason why, in the long run, every society looks like a familiar *bonhomme*. It is also the reason why—if we think about it—every individual seems to be always ready to 'flip out'. By means of parents, teachers, friends and every other 'formative' factor, the child 'interiorizes'—as they say—different and specified positions in society. Leaving aside his personal biopsychic 'baggage'—which is nevertheless there—in any case he necessarily has to put together these different positions within himself and try to shape them into an individual unity. It is therefore true that every individual is the product of his society; but he is inevitably produced as a problem or conflict among different positions within this very society.

The first consequence of this is the concrete and non-utopian differentiation of the individual from the society that nonetheless generated him. Not only is the individual not generated as a waste, or residual shadow of social totality, he is also generated as a distinct pole which therefore has the potential to object to this very totality. Such a differentiation tends strongly to decrease only when it is society itself that takes charge of the individual composition. This is what happens in archaic societies, with their initiatory rituals for every stage of life—or in the case that a single social position is interiorized in a prevailing way, so that there is no longer a problem about individual composition and unification.[25]

If we leave aside these extreme cases, the difficulties and urgencies of this unification imply various modes of repositioning and distancing. The emergence of the *unconscious* could be considered as the first and most fundamental of them, with its characteristic methods of proceeding, which entail at the same time—for better or worse—an extraordinary development and anchoring. But these

25 This is the most serious problem one faces in every totalitarian society or tendency. Every form of totalitarianism we currently know of has never managed radically to destroy the creation of differences and hence the possibility of individual resistance. But totalitarianism is already as such an index of a reduction of these differences; this is also the most dangerous index, with respect to which ethical warnings do not count much.

methods do not as such belong only to the individual. Precisely insofar as there is no substantial difference between individual and society, when facing particularly difficult problems, they also appear in society—in spite of the basic mitigation offered by the possibility of distributing across the manifold what the individual needs to gather within himself. For instance, it is unlikely that a society could become thoroughly obsessive—we saw this in the case of archaic societies. But it is equally the case that we are compelled to acknowledge clear obsessive traits in some societies, just as we find in an obsessional the microscopic kernel of an archaic society.

In this way, moving from specific problems faced by individuals and societies in completely different situations, it is possible to outline types of solutions that are homogeneous with one another, in spite of the at-times-enormous gap between their premises and circumstances. This is what allowed us to associate obsessive 'illness' with archaic societies and a sociopolitical movement of the twentieth century.[26]

A GENETIC CELL

At this stage, we should address the implications of the configuration we isolated—which is certainly one among many that research will be able to identify and modulate. Undoubtedly, it delineates a dynamic centre, from which a particular movement—whether individual or collective—is originated; in this sense, it appears to be a matrix or genetic cell which, however, disregards that immense accumulation of facts, experience, conquests and defeats that make history—as we often say—'unrepeatable'. Instead, this configuration implies the possibility of repeating, across abysmal distances, a given and well-defined quality of the course of history, of producing segments of

26 In this way, it is really possible to overcome the difference in approach Freud noted, in *Totem and Taboo*, between his research ('applying the point of view and the findings of psycho-analysis to some unsolved problems of social psychology') and Carl Gustav Jung's ('solv[ing] the problems of individual psychology with the help of material derived from social psychology')— *SE*, VOL. 13, p. *xiii* / *GW*, VOL. 9, p. 3.

history or individual life in which we are obliged to recognize a common fundamental characteristic. This does not rule out but actually reinforces historical distinctness in the strict sense.

POSSIBLE AND IMPOSSIBLE HISTORIES

We are thus led to question history. From what we have said so far, it is clear that the notion of History as an irreversible flux and a one-way totalization in which every previous process is absorbed enters into crisis. It is not only History as 'the princely progress of the human race' that enters into crisis. Concerning this progress, the events of the twentieth century forced us to open our eyes. What is additionally in crisis is the totalitarian and homogenizing conception of historical *time* and historical processes that arguably constitutes the ideological heaven of Western civilization.

There exist different historical times and spatial curvatures in which human vicissitudes take place; in place of a linear unfolding, we should think of more lines and particular logics that intersect in various ways with respect to different and even recurrent problems, following very specific temporal rhythms. This is why, under certain conditions, we see the emergence of unheard-of developments that come centre stage, or developments which we forgot about or thought impossible. There are also developments that intend radically to abolish history, or sacralize it; paradoxically, by interfering with others of a different nature, at times they give rise to actual climaxes of history. In the end, elaborating on the words of a professional historian, history is not only the 'total of all possible histories'[27] but also the sum of *impossible* histories.

This condition refers us back to that dyadic structure we discussed in Chapter II. In the archaic world, which is only apparently solid and complete, the spirit of Prometheus is present; time as a closed circularity is eventually outdone by linear time, which mythically began with the Titan's run that brought the divine fire from heaven to earth. Reciprocally, today Prometheus sees the rise of the

27 Fernand Braudel, *On History* (Chicago: University of Chicago Press, 1982), p. 34.

anti-Prometheus who contrasts him; the time of the shot arrow is interrupted and deviated by the (perhaps always more numerous) attempts at reinstating archaic time. From this perspective—which is undoubtedly a long-term one—an examination of contemporary historical movements may turn out to be remarkably surprising.

For example, we may find that explicitly revolutionary movements, open to the future, are actually in an ambiguous position with regard to time, or better, are *poly-temporal*. There is here a richness and availability which, if unrecognized and suffocated by the pre-eminence of the future, runs the risk of being transformed into an extremely serious internal difficulty. The *redemption* of history that enlivens these movements then turns into an attempted *suppression*; there emerge collective realities that are generally immobile, strongly ritualized and subjected to an absolute authority—which in many respects recall archaic realities. Here there is no deviation or degeneration with regard to the origins—that is, the purely revolutionary project—as we often tend to think; instead, there is a coming out in the open and absolutization of something that was readable even earlier, at the starting point.

We may also find that the more intense the insistence towards a rupture of the archaic circle, the more intensely opposite tendencies prevail. The French Revolution decapitates kings and establishes the cult of Reason as a deity; the Russian Revolution abolishes private property and embalms Lenin. In this light, the events of our century force us to carry out a lucid and detailed examination of the revolutionary attempts at blasting 'the continuum of history'.[28] Half a century ago, Walter Benjamin criticized the 'social democratic' conception of history, because it was bound to 'dogmatic claims' about the concept of progress and an idea of the historical process as a 'homogenous, empty time'.[29] It is easy to agree with that. But

28 Walter Benjamin, 'On the Concept of History' in *Selected Writings, Volume 4: 1938-1940* (Cambridge MA: Harvard University Press, 2006), p. 395. In this context, see also Giorgio Agamben, 'Time and History' in *Infancy and History. The Destruction of Experience* (London: Verso, 1993), pp. 89–106.

29 Benjamin, 'On the Concept of History', pp. 394–5.

Benjamin put forward his critique from the standpoint of a history based on a mythical alliance between historical materialism and theology, a history seen as 'the subject of a construction whose site is not homogeneous, empty time, but time filled full by now-time [*Jetztzeit*]'.[30] He insisted on discontinuity and the break with the mechanical time of clocks, on the absolute beginning given at the instant of revolutionary action which is necessarily indistinguishable from this very action; all this points at the coming to the fore of a time 'shot through with splinters of messianic time'.[31] This sacralization of time and history, here outlined at its dawn, has also been lived in its subsequent developments which assumed those characteristics of arrest or end of history in the archaic sense we mentioned.

For this reason, we are compelled to see in Benjamin's words only *one* of the aspects of the Promethean dyad. They indicate the necessity to seize, in every individual or collective experience, *all* the implicated temporalities, without forgetting any, or better, without declaring the abolishment of any of them by means of a political or cultural legislative decree. Here we are approaching another point that emerges from our investigation.

CHRONOTYPY

This point concerns the very method we have adopted so far. As we saw, within psychoanalytic practice, I was struck by a totally unusual behaviour with respect to time. Time's annulment turned out to be related to the problematic knot defined by an individual experience. Now, the annulment of time, following different procedures, can also be found in other situations, alien to the psychoanalytic field; I was therefore persuaded to examine some of them. Holding fast to the thread of time, I clarified problems and difficulties that are apparently completely different from one another. Little by little, I singled out a common genetic cell, which, however, does not abolish the

30 Benjamin, 'On the Concept of History', p. 395.

31 Benjamin, 'On the Concept of History', p. 397.

ineradicable differences that exists among the various situations. On the contrary, it was precisely the examination of these differences that enabled me to put forward some hypotheses—which I hope are robust enough—in the context of the controversial relationship between individual and society.

Thus, I have not formulated, so to speak, 'transversal' generalities, such as those pursued by so-called interdisciplinary research—when it is not limited to the ritual evocations of scholars entrenched in their disciplines. Instead, it seems to me that I have individuated an *element that orders* both individual and collective events, namely, time: I have followed one of its well-characterized adventures and noticed that a particular nexus of events is arranged around it, in situations that are completely disconnected. From this standpoint, the genetic cell is first and foremost a particular *chronotype*. I do not know whether there are other ordering elements of this kind; but I believe that the presence of just one of them actually allows us to reach a multi-layered working hypothesis. It is up to others to assess whether the use of this method involves, in my case, a real improvement; for me, it seems in any case to contain a general indication.

Let us take a step back. Freud assembled and refined a kind of knowledge about obsessionals that, in his time, belonged to individual psychopathology. In doing so, he realized that this knowledge interacted, in a surprising way, with the one assembled by anthropologists about archaic societies. At this point, he attempted a synthesis or unification that, on the one hand, appeared substantially alien to psychoanalysts and, on the other, seemed incongruous or mythological to anthropologists. In my opinion, it was instead both premature and lacking an incontestable founding principle. This founding principle could be time. Through an examination of its elaboration, we indeed attain something that obsessionals and archaic people share, and understand why this is the case. In addition, we attain something that enables us to build a bridge towards the historical experience of a contemporary society.

I think it is by now clear to any unbiased reader that what is at stake here is not an attempt to occupy territories that are deemed to remain separate but, rather, a process of slow and strenuous scientific unification. As always, the latter involves a cognitive simplification of the whole set, together with a different reading of the various subsets that compose it. (For this approach based on the ordering element of time, I am tempted to suggest the term *chronotypy*; just as the linotypist is a worker who creates lines of writing by typing letters of a certain font, so the chronotypist would be the one who, by using a given chronotype or temporal font, brings together various events into a characteristic series . . .)

If I am not wrong, there could arise here a way of considering human action, whether individual or collective, capable of stimulating a reformulation of the various partial sciences that already exist about it.

Appendix

ON FREUD'S *VERLEUGNUNG*

The process of repudiation of death to which are connected the attempts at an elaboration of time we have described is in turn related to the concept of *Verleugnung* (which is usually rendered as 'denial' or 'disavowal'). The latter becomes quite important in the late Freud, yet so far seems to have been mostly overlooked. It is worth summarizing its development in Freud's work and its subsequent ramifications.

Verleugnung initially unfolds through modalities that recall those of the later concept of *Verneinung* (negation). For example, Freud speaks of the *Verleugnung* of unpleasant memories that emerged during psychoanalysis[1] and, correlatively, of *Ableugnen*, or 'disowning', in relation to the actual forgetting of unpleasant memories;[2] or also of the *Verleugnung* of guilt, or of an attributed misdeed.[3] This meaning is still present in his later work; for instance, in the lectures of 1915–17, he refers to the *Verleugnung* of tendencies that become manifest through the interpretation of dreams.[4] And yet this meaning tends gradually to give way to that of repudiation or denial of *an element of reality*. Something unbearable perceived in reality is forcefully repelled and refused.

1 Josef Breuer and Sigmund Freud, *Studies on Hysteria* in *SE*, VOL. 2, p. 289 / *GW*, VOL. 1, p. 282.

2 Sigmund Freud, *The Psychopathology of Everyday Life* in *SE*, VOL. 6, p. 144 / *GW*, VOL. 4, pp. 160–2.

3 Sigmund Freud, 'Psycho-Analysis and the Establishment of the Facts in Legal Proceedings' in *SE*, VOL. 9, p. 113 / *GW*, VOL. 7, p. 13.

4 Sigmund Freud, *Introductory Lectures on Psycho-Analysis* in *SE*, VOL. 15, p. 144 / *GW*, VOL. 11, p. 145.

In this sense, the difference between *Verleugnung* and *Verneinung* becomes increasingly clearer—the latter stands for a process of negation of a repressed element that emerges in consciousness, that is, an element *internal* to the psychic apparatus. At the same time, *Verleugnung* is also increasingly differentiated from repression in the strict sense (*Verdrängung*), namely, the process of expelling into or maintaining within the unconscious an element bound to the drives and the *internal* thrusts of the organism. While in 1911 *Verleugnung* amounts to the 'most extreme type' of separation from reality carried out through the process of repression,[5] it later becomes a 'mechanism analogous' to that of repression,[6] only to be further specified as a defence against the claims of reality, whereas repression is a defence against the internal claims related to the drive.[7]

This is therefore Freud's final stance on an issue—the rejection of reality—that acquires an increasing importance in his work.

What is the reason for the growing attention Freud pays to *Verleugnung*? According to Laplanche and Pontalis,[8] we should first and foremost see it as related to Freud's constant desire to find a mechanism of defence specific to psychosis. It is beyond doubt that such a desire is explicitly manifested in several texts. But the significance the authors of the *Vocabulaire* attribute to the theme of psychosis seems more connected with a stage of Lacan's investigations than with Freud's own approach. Lacan in fact isolates in some texts, especially the clinical case history of the 'Wolfman',[9] the process of

5 Sigmund Freud, 'Formulations on the Two Principles of Mental Functioning' in *SE*, VOL. 12, p. 218 / *GW*, VOL. 8, pp. 230–1.

6 Sigmund Freud, 'Neurosis and Psychosis' in *SE*, VOL. 19, pp. 149–53 / *GW*, VOL. 13, pp. 387–91.

7 Sigmund Freud, 'An Outline of Psycho-Analysis' in *SE*, VOL. 23, pp. 202–03 / *GW*, VOL. 17, pp. 133–4.

8 Jean Laplanche and Jean-Bertrand Pontalis, *The Language of Psychoanalysis* (London: Karnac Books, 1988), pp. 81–2, pp. 166–9.

9 Sigmund Freud, *From the History of an Infantile Neurosis* in *SE*, VOL. 17, pp. 7–122 / *GW*, VOL. 12, pp. 29–157.

Verwerfung (*forclusion* in French; *preclusione* in Italian) as typical of psychosis. A careful examination of Lacan's operation enables us to see—beneath his occasional forcing of the text[10]—that *Verwerfung* is

10 Lacan explicitly relies on two passages from Freud (Jacques Lacan, *Écrits* [New York-London: Norton, 2006], pp. 322–4). First: '*Eine Verdrängung ist etwas anderes als eine Verwerfung*' (*GW*, VOL. 12, p. 111); 'A repression is something different from a *Verwerfung*'. This is Freud's final deliberation on the fact that the child under consideration rejected, because of his fear of castration, the explanation of sexual intercourse as involving the vagina and kept to the previous explanation based on anal penetration. From this followed for the child a logical contradiction between the fear of castration and the identification with woman through the bowels. But, indeed, we are here facing 'only a logical contradiction, which does not mean much. The whole process is actually typical of the way in which the unconscious works. A repression is something different from a *Verwerfung*'. Here Freud identifies the *Verwerfung* with a refusal that is unfolded on the conscious level and therefore leads to the elimination of the logical contradiction, while the *Verdrängung*, which is unfolded in the unconscious, preserves the two contrasting terms. The Italian translator (*Opere*, VOL. 7, p. 553) renders the passage like the French translator anathematized by Lacan, and interprets *Verwerfung* as 'conscious repudiation [*ripudio cosciente*]'. Second: '[. . .] *ist die nächste Bedeutung dieses Ausdrucks, dass er von ihr nichts wissen wollte im Sinne der Verdrängung. Damit war eigentlich kein Urteil über ihre Existenz gefällt, aber es war so gut, als ob sie nicht existierte*' (*GW*, VOL. 12, p. 117). 'The most immediate meaning of this expression [*Verwerfung* of castration] is that he did not want to know anything in the sense of repression. With this an actual judgment on [its] existence was not formulated, but in the end it was as if it did not exist.' Here Freud highlights the intensity of the procedure through which the child rejects, *verwirft*, castration and keeps to the theory of anal intercourse. The expression 'he did not want to know anything in the sense of repression', on which Lacan relies, is rather ambiguous, and can lend itself to both Lacan's version (that is, an opposition between *Verwerfung* and *Verdrängung*) and the one provided in the Italian translation (*Opere*, VOL. 7, p. 558): 'He did not want to know anything about it, that is, he repressed it [*non ne volle sapere affatto, e cioè la rimosse*]'. However, an examination of the context rules out Lacan's opposition and simply highlights the existence of a 'third trend', older than the two antithetical ones (horror of castration and its acceptance by means of a compensatory identification with woman). This 'third trend' was limited to rejecting castration without even addressing the issue of a judgment on its existence. We can see that Lacan's isolation of *Verwerfung* as distinct from *Verdrängung* is arbitrary. However, what is not arbitrary is the isolation of a procedure of *als ob*, doing *as if* something did not exist. This is the

actually connected in a direct way with that branch of research which, a few years after the case study of the 'Wolfman', leads Freud to identify the process of *Verleugnung*. In other words, what Lacan names *Verwerfung*, and considers as a typical procedure of psychosis, is something Freud calls *Verleugnung* around 1925–27 and involves a much wider problem. The reason for Freud's focusing on this issue has thus not only to do with the problem of psychosis as opposed to neurosis but, rather, with the more general problem of the rejection of reality and its replacement with a new reality,[11] which is carried out in a way that clearly exceeds the schema elaborated for neurosis (that is, repression of the drive and return of the repressed in the guise of symptom).

Like repression, *Verleugnung* is initially a normal process, or at least it has a normal prototype. As early as 1911, Freud speaks of an intentional *Verleugnung* of reality, caused by the desire to sleep. Here *Verleugnung* forms the presupposition for the restoration in sleep of the 'likeness of mental life as it was before the recognition of reality'.[12] Thus, in this case, the intentional repudiation of reality enables the emergence of a kind of psychic functioning that is exclusively based on the pleasure-unpleasure principle. Oneiric phenomena are in this sense something that appears *after* reality is repudiated.

The same applies to other situations. It is here that the phenomenon of psychosis explicitly intervenes, in the first place that of

procedure Freud will call *Verleugnung*. Among other things, this is proved by the fact that what is here the object of *Verwerfung*, what is being rejected, coincides with one of the fundamental themes of Freud's *Verleugnung* (that is, the disavowal of castration and fetishism; see below). The curious absence of *Verleugnung* in Lacan—at least its absence from the texts collected in *Écrits*—has been noticed also by Ambrogio Ballabio, *Un mito d'origine: del simbolico e/o del reale* [A Myth of the Origin: Of the Symbolic and/or the Real], manuscript (Milan, 1979).

11 Sigmund Freud, 'The Loss of Reality in Neurosis and Psychosis' in *SE*, VOL. 19, pp. 183–90 / *GW*, VOL. 13, pp. 363–68.

12 Freud, 'Formulations on the Two Principles of Mental Functioning' in *SE*, VOL. 12, p. 219 / *GW*, VOL. 8, p. 231.

'hallucinatory psychosis'.[13] Freud later repeatedly returns to this theme in order to distinguish neurosis and psychosis.[14]

But, for Freud, the process of repudiation of reality is also given in another *normal* situation, one that is, at the same time, crucial for his theory, namely, the apprehension of sexual difference through the observation, for both males and females, of the genitals of the other sex. This is the crucial experience in which, for the male, the Oedipal orientation is usually solved, or 'wanes', while for the female it is initiated. Starting from 1908 and up to his last notes of 1938, Freud's descriptions are substantially consistent.

Facing a reality—the fact that little girls do not have a penis—that contradicts his phallic framework ('everybody has it'), the little boy repudiates this reality and tells himself: 'Hers is still quite small. But when she gets bigger it'll grow all right.'[15] Facing the reality of the little boy's penis, the situation is different for the little girl: 'She has seen it [the penis of a brother or playmate] and knows she is without it and wants to have it.'[16] In this case, the repudiation does not concern the genitals of the other sex, but the fact that *she* lacks these genitals. The little girl can therefore directly repudiate castration, while the little boy repudiates it indirectly through the little girl. In both cases, the recognition of castration—which follows the initial repudiation—constitutes the essential element for a normal development. In the male, castration forces him to renounce the mother

13 Freud, 'Formulations on the Two Principles of Mental Functioning', p. 218 / *GW*, VOL. 8, p. 230.

14 See above note 6 on p. 115 and note 11 on p. 117.

15 Sigmund Freud, 'The Sexual Theories of Children' in *SE*, VOL. 9, p. 216 / *GW*, VOL. 7, p. 178; *Analysis of a Phobia in a Five-Year Old Boy* in *SE*, VOL. 10, p. 11 / *GW*, VOL. 7, pp. 249–50; 'The Infantile Genital Organisation: An Interpolation into the Theory of Sexuality' in *SE*, VOL. 19, pp. 141–5 / *GW*, VOL. 13, pp. 293–8.

16 Sigmund Freud, 'Some Psychical Consequences of the Anatomical Distinction Between the Sexes' in *SE*, VOL. 19, pp. 252 / *GW*, VOL. 14, pp. 19-30; 'Female Sexuality' in *SE*, VOL. 21, pp. 229–30 / *GW*, VOL. 14, p. 522; 'Findings, Ideas, Problems' in *SE*, VOL. 23, p. 299 / *GW*, VOL. 17, p. 151.

and gives rise to an identification with the paternal agency (the formation of the superego). This is indeed the 'waning of the Oedipus complex'. In the little girl, renouncing her own penis is followed by the desire to have a baby from the father—through the symbolic equation penis-child. In the first case, a threat of castration is operative; in the second, what happens is an acknowledgment that castration did take place.

Freud's interpretation of fetishism[17] clearly follows the same line of reasoning. The fetishist repudiates the absence of the mother's penis. In his 1927 article on the topic, the claim is categorical, while in his previous remarks there was a fluctuation concerning the identity of the female whose castration is repudiated—either the playmate or the mother.[18] Unlike what occurs in the normal male, this repudiation is perpetuated thanks to the positing of a *replacement* for the missing maternal penis. For the unconscious, this replacement *is* the penis, even though the fetishist knows well that woman actually does not have a penis. The splitting of the ego on which Freud insists later in his work is already outlined here.[19]

It would seem that Freud's applications of the concept of repudiation, *Verleugnung*, are in this way essentially completed. But on close inspection another situation subjected to repudiation emerges—although obliquely, so to speak—one that directly concerns our investigation. This situation is death. Commenting on the case of a girl who became hysterical after the death of her sister, Freud adds: 'the *psychotic* reaction would have been a disavowal of the fact of her

17 Sigmund Freud, 'Fetishism' in *SE*, VOL. 21, pp. 152–9 / *GW*, VOL. 14, pp. 311–17.

18 Sigmund Freud, 'Delusions and Dreams in Jensen's *Gradiva*' in *SE*, VOL. 9, p. 46 ff / *GW*, VOL. 7, p. 73; 'Leonardo da Vinci and a Memory of his Childhood' in *SE*, VOL. 11, pp. 94–5 / *GW*, VOL. 8, pp. 164–5.

19 Sigmund Freud, 'Splitting of the Ego in the Process of Defence' in *SE*, VOL. 23, pp. 275–8 / *GW*, VOL. 17, pp. 59–62; 'An Outline of Psycho-Analysis' in *SE*, VOL. 23, p. 202 / *GW*, VOL. 17, p. 133.

sister's death'.[20] Here the repudiation of death is deemed to be openly psychotic. However, later on, Freud again finds this kind of repudiation in different kinds of situations. He refers to the case of two young neurotics, one of whom was an obsessional, who underwent—with regard to the death of their father—the same process of repudiation and simultaneous recognition that Freud also attributes to the fetishist.[21] Finally, speaking about the Egyptian religion, Freud claims that, unlike Jewish religion, it was very concerned with repudiating death.[22]

From this survey, we can conclude that the *Verleugnung* Freud recovers in numerous situations is not actually a process typical of one of them. In this sense, Freud's use of it is antithetical to the use Lacan makes of *Verwerfung*. Instead, for Freud, *Verleugnung* is typical of the *unbearable character* of a real experience that is presented to the subject, not of a given experience. Moreover, this process does not necessarily have to be accompanied by the splitting of the ego for which, as we saw, the real experience is simultaneously repudiated and recognized.

Moving from these premises, and specifically the interpretation of fetishism, Winnicott described his well-known 'transitional objects and phenomena'.[23] The latter amount to a normal field of experience for the child, placed at the beginning of his separation from the mother. The transitional object symbolizes in fact the union of two beings who are about to be separated. In this situation, there is still

20 Freud, 'The Loss of Reality in Neurosis and Psychosis' in *SE*, VOL. 19, p. 184 / *GW*, VOL. 13, p. 364.

21 Freud, 'Fetishism', pp. 155–6 / *GW*, pp. 315–16.

22 Sigmund Freud, *Moses and Monotheism: Three Essays* in *SE*, VOL. 23, pp. 19–20 / *GW*, VOL. 16, p. 117.

23 Winnicott, 'Transitional Objects and Transitional Phenomena'; 'The Location of Cultural Experience, *International Journal of Psycho-Analysis* 48 (1966): 368–72. In this regard, see also Phyllis Greenacre, 'The Transitional Object and the Fetish with Special Reference to the Role of Illusion', *International Journal of Psycho-Analysis* 51 (1970): 447–56.

an inability to recognize the reality of separation and, at the same time, an increasing ability to do so; the experience of *illusion* is located here, which is permitted to the child and subsequently belongs to the arts, religions and creative life of the adult.

We can see that Freud's research on *Verleugnung* and its use in several circumstances becomes with Winnicott a determination of a normal field of experience, which is backdated, albeit not in an exclusive manner, to the relation to the mother's breast. The coexistence of recognition and disavowal of reality, which is typical of Freud's fetishist, thus becomes the normal field of illusion—and, after all, Freud already identified this issue with regard to religion.[24]

We could say that Winnicott's elaboration provides us with a general framework in which the situations investigated by Freud are inscribed through different modalities. Fetish and normal transitional object can thus be considered as two extreme cases, or poles, that are connected by means of a range of intermediate situations. The difference between them is more or less similar to that between delirium and illusion.[25] Through his clinical experience with adult neurotics, Freud was led to stress the delirium-fetish pole, while, moving from his paediatric experience, Winnicott highlighted the transitional phenomenon-illusion pole.

Going back to the repudiation of death in the sense treated in the present work, it is important to observe that it is naturally included in this field. With respect to the child who will become an obsessional, we postulated a precociously arrested relation of belonging, at the level of Mahler's stage of separation-individuation, or at that of Winnicott's transitional stage (see Chapter IV). As for the archaic group, we described an analogous relation with regard to the value-figure of the group (see Chapter III). Moving from this

24 Sigmund Freud, *The Future of an Illusion* in *SE*, VOL. 21, p. 30 / *GW*, VOL. 14, p. 352 ff.

25 Greenacre, 'The Transitional Object and the Fetish', p. 450 ff.

kind of situation, the obsessional's repudiation of death gives rise to a ritualization that is closer to the fetish pole than to the (normal) one of illusion. In other words, we are dealing with an anxious ritualization that *stands for* the figure that has been threatened with death and intends immediately to witness its presence, just as the fetish intends to witness the missing penis. The archaic repudiation is instead closer to the pole of illusion, that is, the pole where an institutional religion in the strict sense arises. But even in this case there are often clear fetishistic references that reduce the differences.

THE SITTING KING

At Shark Point near Cape Padron, in Lower Guinea, lives the priestly king, Kukulu, alone in a wood. He may not touch a woman nor leave his house; indeed he may not even quit his chair, in which he is obliged to sleep sitting, for if he lay down no wind would arise and navigation would be stopped. He regulates storms, and in general maintains a wholesome and equable state of the atmosphere.[26]

26 Adolf Bastian, *Die deutsche Expedition an der Loango-Küste*, VOL. 1 (Jena: Hermann Costenoble, 1874–75), p. 287. Quoted in James George Frazer, *The Golden Bough: A Study in Comparative Religion* [New York/ London: MacMillan, 1894], p. 108; and in Freud, *Totem and Taboo*, *SE*, VOL. 13, p. 45.

Index of Names